First World War

and Army of Occupation

War Diary

France, Belgium and Germany

GUARDS DIVISION
4 Guards Brigade
Irish Guards
2nd Battalions
1 February 1918 - 31 October 1918

WO95/1226/3

The Naval & Military Press Ltd
www.nmarchive.com
Published in association with The National Archives

Published by

The Naval & Military Press Ltd

Unit 10 Ridgewood Industrial Park,

Uckfield, East Sussex,

TN22 5QE England

Tel: +44 (0) 1825 749494

www.naval-military-press.com

www.nmarchive.com

This diary has been reprinted in facsimile from the original. Any imperfections are inevitably reproduced and the quality may fall short of modern type and cartographic standards.

Contents

Document type	Place/Title	Date From	Date To
Heading	1226/3 2nd Bttn Irish Guards Feb-Oct 1918		
Heading	31st Division 4th Gds Bde 2nd Bn Irish Gds 1918 Feb-1918 Oct Diaries For 1915 July-1918-Jan 1918, Nov-1919 Jan With 2 Guards Bde Attached 31 Div.		
Heading	Confidential War Diary of 2nd Battalion Irish Guards Vol. II, 1918 Period From Feb. 1st To Feb. 28th,1918. Vol 31.		
War Diary	Support Lines	01/02/1918	03/02/1918
War Diary	Front Line	03/02/1918	04/02/1918
War Diary	Line	05/02/1918	06/02/1918
War Diary	Arras	06/02/1918	12/02/1918
War Diary	Bray	12/02/1918	17/02/1918
War Diary	Bailleul-Willerval Line (support)	18/02/1918	19/02/1918
War Diary	Support	20/02/1918	20/02/1918
War Diary	Support To Front Line	21/02/1918	21/02/1918
War Diary	Front Line	22/02/1918	24/02/1918
War Diary	Line Ecurie	25/02/1918	25/02/1918
Miscellaneous	Ecurie	26/02/1918	28/02/1918
Heading	31th Division 4th Guards Brigade War Diary 2nd Battalion The Irish Guards March 1918		
War Diary	Ecurie Wood Camp Stuart Camp.	01/03/1918	01/03/1918
Miscellaneous	A.29.b.5.3.	01/03/1918	03/03/1918
War Diary	Farbus Line	04/03/1918	09/03/1918
War Diary	Villers Brulin	09/03/1918	24/03/1918
War Diary	Ervillers Area	24/03/1918	25/03/1918
War Diary	Courcelles ridge	25/03/1918	26/03/1918
War Diary	Ayette	26/03/1918	31/03/1918
Heading	4th Guards Brigade 31st Division 2nd Battalion The Irish Guards April 1918.		
War Diary	Bienvillers To Sombrin	01/04/1918	01/04/1918
War Diary	Sombrin To Chelers	02/04/1918	02/04/1918
War Diary	Chelers	03/04/1918	19/04/1918
War Diary	Line	20/04/1918	30/04/1918
War Diary	Hondeghem	01/05/1918	19/05/1918
War Diary	Form Hondeghem-Bacly Wood	20/05/1918	21/05/1918
War Diary	Barly Camp (p.26)	21/05/1918	23/05/1918
War Diary	Bary Camp	24/05/1918	29/05/1918
War Diary	Barly	30/05/1918	31/05/1918
Miscellaneous	Wo On 8/2/18 4/99. 3/c.g	08/02/1918	08/02/1918
Heading	Guards Division 4th Gds Bde 2nd Bn Irish Gds June-Oct. 1918		
War Diary	Barly Camp	01/06/1918	11/06/1918
War Diary	Bavincourt	11/06/1918	30/06/1918
War Diary	Confidential War Diary of 2nd Irish Guards. Vol. VII, 1918 From : 1st July, 1918 To. 31st July, 1918.		
War Diary	Bavincourt	01/07/1918	04/07/1918
War Diary	Kuly Bavin Court	05/07/1918	06/07/1918
War Diary	Bavin Court	07/07/1918	09/07/1918
War Diary	Criel Plage	10/07/1918	31/07/1918

Miscellaneous	Report On The Ceremonial Parade In Paris, British Composite Battalion July 10th-July 16th,1918.	10/07/1918	10/07/1918
Heading	War Diary 2nd. Bn. Irish Guards. Volume. VIII (1918.) Period:- August 1st. To 31st. 1918.		
War Diary	Criel Plage	01/08/1918	31/08/1918
Heading	Confidential War Diary of 2nd Bn, Irish Guards Vol. IX, 1918. Period: From 1st Sept. To 30th Sept. 1918.		
War Diary	Criel Plage	01/09/1918	30/09/1918
Heading	Confidential War Diary of 2nd Battalion, Irish Guards. Vol. X-1918, Period From 1st October To 31st October, 1918.		
War Diary	Criel Plage	01/10/1918	31/10/1918

1226/3 2nd Bttn Irish Guards

Feb– OCT 1918

31ST DIVISION
4TH GDS BDE

2ND BN IRISH GDS

~~FEB – MAY 1918~~

1918 FEB – 1918 OCT

DIARIES FOR 1915 JULY – 1918 JAN
1918 NOV – 1919 JAN
~~WITH~~ 2 GUARDS BDE

attached 31 DIV

CONFIDENTIAL.

4/31

WAR DIARY

of

2nd Battalion, Irish Guards.

Vol. II, 1918.

Period :

From Feb. 1st

To Feb. 28th, 1918.

1.18

131

(1) Army Form C. 2118.

Instructions regarding War Diaries and Intelligence Summaries are contained in F. S. Regs., Part II. and the Staff Manual respectively. Title pages will be prepared in manuscript.

WAR DIARY or ~~INTELLIGENCE SUMMARY~~.

(Erase heading not required.)

2nd Bn Irish Guards.

Place	Date	Hour	Summary of Events and Information	Remarks and references to Appendices
Support-line	Feb 1918	1st	The Bn was situated in Support. 3 coys in HARRY, HUMID and HUSSAR TRENCHES with one coy in COLT TRENCH. Bn H.Q. in NORTHUMBERLAND AVENUE, a sunken road about 1000 yds behind the line. These support trenches were only fair, with a few dug-outs in them, the remaining accommodation being small trench shelters.	
	Feb	2nd	Usual work of repairing and improving the trenches was carried out during the day — fatigue parties for carrying up rations and material to the front-line, were found at night.	
Front-line	Feb	3rd	At 5.45 pm coys marched up to take over the front line from the 1st Bn COLDSTREAM GUARDS. By 8 pm the relief was complete. The Bn was distributed as follows. 3 companies in the front line and 1 coy in Support. No 3 coy (right) No 4 (centre) No 2 (left) with No 1 coy in support. Except for the shuffling of companies, the Bn held the line exactly the same as during the last tour.	
	Feb	4th	Fine sunny day — practically no shelling. No work of any importance could be done during daylight.	

A7092). Wt. W12839/M1297 750,000. 1/17. D. D & L., Ltd. Forms/C2118/14.

Instructions regarding War Diaries and Intelligence Summaries are contained in F. S. Regs., Part II. and the Staff Manual respectively. Title pages will be prepared in manuscript.

(2) Army Form C. 2118.

WAR DIARY
or
~~INTELLIGENCE SUMMARY.~~
(*Erase heading not required.*)

2nd Bn Irish Guards

Place	Date	Hour	Summary of Events and Information	Remarks and references to Appendices
LINE.	Feb. 1918	5th	another very quiet day – little or no sniping and practically no shell fire except for a few trench mortar shells. About 7 pm the H.Q. of the 1st Bn SCOTS GUARDS arrived, followed by the incoming companies. The relief which ought to have been completed by 10 pm at the latest was held up, owing to the fear of a German gas bombardment of FAMPOUX, with the result that the SCOTS GUARDS had to detrain before reaching that village and then come all the way round PUDDING TR. so as to avoid the village of FAMPOUX. The relief however went off without any difficulties, although the night was dark.	
	Feb 6th		By 2.30 am the whole relief was complete and coys marched independently to the Railway siding, a few hundred yards W of FAMPOUX, via PUDDING TR.	
ARRAS			No 1 and 2 coys got away by an early train. Bn HQ No 3 and 4 coys did not get entrained till after 4 am. At 6 am the whole Bn was in Arras. The billets were the houses at the South end of the town, near the RAILWAY STATION, quite good and comfortable.	

A7092). Wt. W12839/M1293 750,000. 1/17. D. D & L., Ltd. Forms/C2118/14.

Instructions regarding War Diaries and Intelligence Summaries are contained in F. S. Regs., Part II. and the Staff Manual respectively. Title pages will be prepared in manuscript.

(3)

Army Form C. 2118.

WAR DIARY
or
~~INTELLIGENCE SUMMARY.~~
(Erase heading not required.)

2nd Bn Irish Guards.

Place	Date	Hour	Summary of Events and Information	Remarks and references to Appendices
ARRAS	Feb 6th (cont)		Reveille was not till late that morning. The remainder of the day was spent in cleaning equipment, clothes etc.	
" "	Feb 7th		Owing to these billets, only being lent to us, and being required by another Div in whose area we were, the Bn was ordered to move to other billets at the North end of ARRAS. The BEAUMONT BARRACKS were therefore taken over from the 2nd Bn GRENADIER GUARDS, companies starting at 3.30 pm and marching independently. The whole Bn were in the Barracks — Officers messes being in houses close by.	
" "	Feb 8th		Usual routine. Inspection under company arrangements. Baths etc. It poured with rain during the day —.	
" "	Feb 9th		Usual routine. Steady drill, gas helmet drill etc. ~~At 10.30 am The Brigadier (Gen Brooke) said a farewell to Officers & NCOs of the Bn. He was really sorry we were leaving the Division~~	

A7092). Wt. W12839/M1297 750,000. 1/17. D. D & L., Ltd. Forms/C2118/14.

Instructions regarding War Diaries and Intelligence Summaries are contained in F. S. Regs., Part II. and the Staff Manual respectively. Title pages will be prepared in manuscript.

WAR DIARY
or
~~INTELLIGENCE SUMMARY.~~
(Erase heading not required.)

(4)

Army Form C. 2118.

2nd Bn Irish Guards

Place	Date	Hour	Summary of Events and Information	Remarks and references to Appendices
ARRAS.	Feb 10th 1918		Sunday Usual Church parades and services. In the morning the C.O. and 4 coy commanders left ARRAS by motor lorry and proceeded to the H.Q. of 31st Div. Guides took the officers on to the VIMY RIDGE to look over the rear lines of defence and the routes to the SUPPORT LINE. This was arranged prior to the transference of the 4th Guards Bde to the 31st Div.	
			CO & CAPT NUTTING ~~[illegible]~~ dined at the UNIVERSE HOTEL that night with the Brigadier General Brooke commanding 2nd Guards Brigade.	
ARRAS.	Feb 11th		Usual routine in Barracks — steady drill etc. All Bn H.Q. dined at the Universe Hotel in the evening.	
	Feb 12th		In the morning Brig Gen Brooke said goodbye to all the officers & NCOs of the Bn and thanked the Bn for all the good work they had done in the Bde. At 10.12 am The Bn marched out of Barracks, headed by the Band of the Regiment and drums of the 1st Bn Welsh Guards. The Bn marched past our late Brigadier (Gen Brooke) at the RONDE POINT in column of route. Thus we left the Guards Division	

A7092). Wt. W12839/M129² 750,000. 1/17. D. D & L., Ltd. Forms/C2118/14.

Instructions regarding War Diaries and Intelligence Summaries are contained in F. S. Regs., Part II. and the Staff Manual respectively. Title pages will be prepared in manuscript.

(5)

WAR DIARY
or
~~INTELLIGENCE~~ SUMMARY.

(Erase heading not required.)

Army Form C. 2118.

2nd Bn Irish Guards.

Place	Date	Hour	Summary of Events and Information	Remarks and references to Appendices
BRAY.	Feb 12th (cont)		After the march past, corps opened out distance of 200 yds and proceeding via ANZIN, reached BRAY at 12.30 pm The camp consisted of NISSEN huts, Bn H.Q. in a large farm house. A very nice clean camp. Here the Brigade came into Div Reserve.	
" "	Feb 13th		Notification was made that the Corps commander, General McCracken would inspect all the Bns of the 4th Guards Bde in the camps. At 9 am the Bn was paraded for rehearsal. Officers in review order. Bn in Mass. Dress drill order without pouches. Officers in puttees, gloves, without sticks. The drill was good, especially that of the Officers. In the afternoon at 2.30pm all Officers and platoon Sgts attended quite a good lecture on field engineering at ECOVRES.	

A7092) Wt. W12839/M1293 750,000. 1/17. D. D & L. Ltd. Forms/C2118/14.

Instructions regarding War Diaries and Intelligence Summaries are contained in F. S. Regs., Part II. and the Staff Manual respectively. Title pages will be prepared in manuscript.

WAR DIARY
or
~~INTELLIGENCE SUMMARY.~~
(Erase heading not required.)

(6)

Army Form C. 2118.

2nd Bn Irish Guards.

Place	Date	Hour	Summary of Events and Information	Remarks and references to Appendices
BRAY.	Feb	17th	At 9.45 am the Bn marched on parade — the ground chosen was the football ground about ½ mile S of the Camp.	
			By 10 am the Bn was dressed and ready.	
			At 10.15 am the Corps commander stepped from his car and marched onto parade. After the general salute, the General inspected each platoon, walking quickly down the ranks.	
			After the inspection — the Bn marched past in 4s — headed by the drums.	
			The Corps Commander spoke to the C.O. afterwards and complimented the Bn on their smartness and fine physique. He said how honoured he was to have a Guards Brigade in his corps etc.	
			At 3.30 pm. a conference of Commanding Officers was held at Bde H.Q. to discuss the coming tour in the line and other points.	
			At 6 pm the CO held a conference of coy commanders to discuss these points in detail.	

A7092. Wt. W128 9/M1293. 750,000. 1/17. D. D & L. Ltd. Forms/C2118/14.

Instructions regarding War Diaries and Intelligence Summaries are contained in F. S. Regs., Part II. and the Staff Manual respectively. Title pages will be prepared in manuscript.

WAR DIARY
or
~~INTELLIGENCE SUMMARY.~~
(Erase heading not required.)

(7)

Army Form C. 2118.

2nd Bn Irish Guards

Place	Date	Hour	Summary of Events and Information	Remarks and references to Appendices
BRAY	Feb	15th	at 8.30 am the C.O. 4 company commanders and all platoon sgts left ECOIVRES RAILWAY STATION and trained by DECAUVILLE to DAYLIGHT RAILHEAD (VIMY RIDGE). The party then proceeded via TIRED ALLEY (Trench) to the BAILLEUL-WILLERVAL LINE to look over the line held by the 15th Bn WEST YORKS in SUPPORT. The officers were given lunch by the Bn Commander (Lt Col Carter) and the line, approaches etc were carefully looked at and details of the relief arranged between commanders concerned. Party arrived back in BRAY CAMP at 5 pm.	
"	" Feb	16th	Usual routine — of drill, musketry, bayonet fighting etc. In the afternoon the final of the inter coy soccer was played. HQ v No 3 coy. This was won by H.Q. by 3 goals to 0. The C.O. scoring for Bn H.Q.	

A7092. Wt. W1289/M1293. 750,000. 1/17. D. D & L. Ltd. Forms/C2118/14.

Instructions regarding War Diaries and Intelligence Summaries are contained in F. S. Regs., Part II. and the Staff Manual respectively. Title pages will be prepared in manuscript.

WAR DIARY
or
~~INTELLIGENCE SUMMARY.~~
(Erase heading not required.)

(8)

Army Form C. 2118.

2nd Bn Irish Guards.

Place	Date	Hour	Summary of Events and Information	Remarks and references to Appendices
BRAY	Feb 1918	17th	Left BRAY CAMP at 6.45 am, marched to ECOIVRES ST. where the Bn entrained. 35 men per truck in 3 trains. Train started at 7.30 am arriving at DAYLIGHT RAILHEAD at 9 am. Guides were waiting for the coys at this point. Coys marched independently into the line. No 1 coy via TOMMY ALLEY to SUGAR POST. No 2 via TIRED ALLEY to WILLERVAL SOUTH POST. No 4 coy to WILLERVAL NORTH POST. No 3 coy in the line between No 2 & 4 coys and Bn H.Q. all by TIRED. This support line is a continuous line with 3 strong points in it. Everything went smoothly and by 2 pm the whole relief was complete.	
BAILLEUL — WILLERVAL LINE (SUPPORT)	Feb	18th	Day beautifully fine — no shelling. The line being in most places out of view and 1000 yds or more behind the front line. At 11 am the CO was in ARLEUX LOOP when one of our fighting planes was attacked by 4 Bosche — it caught fire at 10,000 ft and crashed 20 yds inside the trench. Although an effort was made to rescue the pilot, all hope was gone, as he was burned to death before reaching the ground.	

A7092. Wt. W12839/M1293. 750,000. 1/17. D. D & L. Ltd. Forms/C2118/14.

Instructions regarding War Diaries and Intelligence Summaries are contained in F. S. Regs., Part II. and the Staff Manual respectively. Title Pages will be prepared in manuscript.

WAR DIARY
or
INTELLIGENCE SUMMARY
(Erase heading not required.)

Army Form C. 2118.

Place	Date	Hour	Summary of Events and Information	Remarks and references to Appendices
BAILLEUL WILLERVAL LINE.	Feb 19th 1918.		Day passed quietly. Work was done in the line to improve it. at 2.30 pm the C.O. went to Bn H.Q. of the 4th Bn GRENADIER GUARDS to look over the front line. The posts in the front line were all visited carefully by moonlight. The night was suspiciously quiet about 8 pm. At 9 am the enemy suddenly opened a terrific bombardment along the whole Brigade front, and followed this up by a strong raiding party of 60 men and an officer. Although the Germans succeeded in entering the line, they were driven out, many being killed & wounded. The Bn on the S.O.S going up, at once stood to and took up our battle positions. which included the coys in the 3 strong points, manning groups of shell holes, both in front & behind their posts, with sections of L. Guns, as well as finding the Garrison of the posts. The 3 coys (mobile) were ready to go up and reinforce the front line Bn in ARLEUX LOOP. In 20 mins the Bn was completely ready for all emergencies in their battle positions. S.O.S. cancelled was sent through from Bde at 11.30 pm, when Bn took up their usual positions as before.	

2449 Wt. W14957/M90 750,000 1/16 J.B.C. & A. Forms/C.2118/12.

Instructions regarding War Diaries and Intelligence Summaries are contained in F. S. Regs., Part II. and the Staff Manual respectively. Title pages will be prepared in manuscript.

WAR DIARY

or

~~INTELLIGENCE SUMMARY.~~ 2nd Bn Irish Guards

(10)

(Erase heading not required.)

Army Form C. 2118.

Place	Date	Hour	Summary of Events and Information	Remarks and references to Appendices
Support.	Feb 1918	20th	Misty morning which turned to a slight drizzle during the afternoon. Coy Commanders proceeded up the line to make detailed arrangements for the relief. During the 4 days in support the Bn did a good deal of digging on a trench to join up SUGAR POST & WILLERVAL SOUTH, so as to make it a continuous and deep trench.	
Support to Front line	Feb	21st	In the morning the 3rd Bn COLDSTREAM GUARDS took over the Support line from the Bn relief being completed by 12 noon. The Bn then proceeded by coys to the front line to take over from the 4th Bn GRENADIER GUARDS. By 3 pm this relief was complete except for the coy relieving ARLEUX POST and the forward platoon for OAK POST, which could not be relieved until dark, owing to the shallowness of the trenches. By 7 pm the whole Bn had taken over the front system, coys being distributed as follows. No 1 coy (right) in TOMMY POST No 4 coy (centre) ARLEUX POST, No 2 coy (left) in OAK POST, and No 3 coy (support) in ARLEUX LOOP.	
Front line.	Feb	22nd	Day fine and quiet — all work had to be done at night — this consisted in clearing and digging out BARRON TRENCH and BRITANNIA, general work on posts and improving communication between the small posts in ARLEUX POST, wiring etc	

A7092). Wt. W12839/M1293 750,000. 1/17. D. D & L. Ltd. Forms/C2118/14.

Instructions regarding War Diaries and Intelligence Summaries are contained in F. S. Regs., Part II. and the Staff Manual respectively. Title Pages will be prepared in manuscript.

WAR DIARY
or
~~INTELLIGENCE SUMMARY~~
(Erase heading not required.)

2nd Bn Irish Guards.

(11)

Army Form C. 2118.

Place	Date	Hour	Summary of Events and Information	Remarks and references to Appendices
Front line.	Feb 22nd (contd)		During the early hours of the morning an urgent telegram had been sent to Bn H.Q. to say that an enemy relief was expected and that identification was urgently needed — consequently strong offensive patrols were sent out by No 2 & 1 Coys to try and scupper enemy patrols in No man's land. These were unsuccessful — but at 4 am a Boche deserter came into our lines at OAK POST. This being most opportune, he was immediately dispatched to Bde H.Q. with a message bearing "Herewith".	
" "	Feb 23rd		Except for slight enemy trench mortar fire, the day passed quietly — much wire was put out on the Bn front and work on trenches completed. Coys took the opportunity, owing to the quietness of the night and distance of the Boche (400 yds approx) to train young officers & N.C.O.s, and men in patrolling. On either flank the next Bdes were at least 700 yds away — so liaison patrols were sent out overnight with an officer to gain touch.	
" "	Feb. 24th		Day quiet & fine. Usual work and patrolling carried out by all companies.	

2449 Wt. W14957/M90 750,000 1/16 J.B.C. & A. Forms/C.2118/12.

(12)

Instructions regarding War Diaries and Intelligence Summaries are contained in F. S. Regs., Part II. and the Staff Manual respectively. Title pages will be prepared in manuscript.

WAR DIARY
or
~~INTELLIGENCE SUMMARY.~~
(Erase heading not required.)

Army Form C. 2118.

2nd Bn Irish Guards

Place	Date	Hour	Summary of Events and Information	Remarks and references to Appendices
Line — ECURIE	Feb 1918	25th ~~19th~~	The Bn was relieved in the morning by the 3rd Bn COLDSTREAM GUARDS. Except for No 4 coy in ARLEUX POST and 1 platoon of No 2 coy in OAK POST who could not be relieved until dark, the relief was completed by 1.30 pm. The Bn marched back — coys independently to ECURIE CAMP — except No 3 coy which went to BRIERLY HILL, to be there for 4 days and to find digging fatigues at night. By 5 pm the Bn less No 3 coy, No 4 coy & 1 platoon No 2 coy was in ECURIE CAMP, where we were in Brigade Reserve. No 4 coy & platoon No 2 coy arrived in camp about 10.30 pm. The Camp consisted of Nissen huts, lined with felt.	J.H.R. Alexander Lt Col Commanding 2nd Bn Irish Guards
ECURIE	Feb	26th	During the morning companies were left at the disposal of company commanders for inspections etc. During the afternoon the C.O. paid a visit to No 3 coy	
	Feb	27th	Mornings work — drill, gas helmet drill etc under coy arrangements. Inter coy football match also Bn drummers v drummers of 3rd C Gds	
	Feb	28th	Heavy rain in the early morning. Morning programme — drill, gas drill — practice patrol formations — baths all day. 2.30 pm football match. Bn XI v Balloon Section result 1—0 a win for us.	

A7092). Wt. W12839/M1293 750,000. 1/17. D. D & L., Ltd. Forms/C2118/14.

31st Division.

4th Guards Brigade.

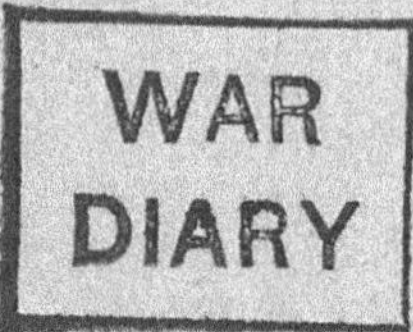

2nd BATTALION

THE IRISH GUARDS

MARCH 1918

Instructions regarding War Diaries and Intelligence Summaries are contained in F. S. Regs., Part II, and the Staff Manual respectively. Title pages will be prepared in manuscript.

WAR DIARY
or
INTELLIGENCE SUMMARY.
(Erase heading not required.)

Army Form C. 2118. (1)

2nd Batt. IRISH GUARDS.

Place	Date 1918 MARCH	Hour	Summary of Events and Information	Remarks and references to Appendices
ECURIE WOOD CAMP – STUART CAMP. A.29.b.5.3.	1st		The Battn left ECURIE WOOD CAMP at 11 a.m. handing over to the K.O.Y.L.I. and marched to STUART CAMP (A.29.b.5.3); the MAJOR-GENERAL watching the Bn march past en route.	MAP REF 51B N.W. 1.20.000.
			The COMDG OFFICER left the Bn to take over temporary command of the 4th GUARDS BRIGADE, the Battn coming under the command of MAJOR LONG-INNES.	
			83 men of the HOUSEHOLD BATTN joined the Bn at STUART CAMP.	
	2nd		In the morning every available officer & man was employed on wiring fatigues under R.E. – Very cold & heavy snow all day.	
			In the afternoon the C.O. was sent for by the MAJOR-GENERAL, who informed him that the Bn must move ~~tomorrow~~ the next day to other camps & dugouts for work in digging & improving the BROWN LINE; final instructions were received at 12 mid. 2nd/3rd.	
	3rd		The Battn marched out at 1.30 p.m. with the exception of No 4 Coy, orders having been received that they were to remain behind temporarily.	
			Bn HdQrs to ECURIE WOOD TRANSPORT LINES (A.27.d.2.4), No 1 Coy to CURRAGH CAMP (B.19.a.2.7) No 2 to FARBUS–WILLERVAL ROAD (B.8.b.5.8). No 3 to RAILWAY LINE (B.21.a.8.3).	
			The Bn now came under the orders of the CORPS, the remainder of the 4th GUARDS BDE having proceeded to DIV. REST in the VILLERS BRULIN area. –	
			The Bn was employed during this & the following days in digging & improving the BROWN or FARBUS LINE. Work was difficult owing to ^direct^ observation by the enemy & constant shelling, all work having to be done in dusk or darkness. Very good work however was done by	

D. D. & L., London, E.C. (A8104) Wt W1771/M2031 750,000 5/17 Sch. 52 Forms/C2118/14

Instructions regarding War Diaries and Intelligence Summaries are contained in F. S. Regs., Part II. and the Staff Manual respectively. Title pages will be prepared in manuscript.

WAR DIARY
or
INTELLIGENCE SUMMARY.
(Erase heading not required.)

Army Form C. 2118. (2)

2nd Bn IRISH GUARDS.

Place	Date 1918	Hour	Summary of Events and Information	Remarks and references to Appendices
FARBUS LINE.	MARCH		the Bn during this period, & the CORPS expressed their satisfaction of this.	
	4th		Work on FARBUS LINE continues. During the day No 4 Coy moved up to dug outs in the RAILWAY CUTTING (B.26.b.8.4).	
	5th		Work on FARBUS LINE continued	
	6th		Ditto.	
	7th		Ditto.	
	8th		Ditto.	
	9th		The Bn was replaced by the 4th Bn GRENADIER GUARDS, & proceeded by train from ECURIE STATION to TINCQUES (C.12.b.3.4) & marched to billets arriving 9.30 p.m. Bn HdQrs & No 1 & 2 Coys in VILLERS-BRULIN, & No 3 & 4 in BETHONSART.	MAP REF. 51c 1.40,000
VILLERS-BRULIN.			The COMDG OFFICER met the Bn at TINCQUES & took over command of the Bn.	LENS 11. 1/100,000
	10th		The day was spent in general cleaning up & inspection by Coys.	
	11th		A lecture was given to the Bn by an officer of the R.F.C. on "Cooperation with aeroplanes" & Coys were otherwise at the disposal of Coy. Comdrs.	
	12th		Adjutants Parade & Spring Shoes.	
	13th		The MAJOR-GENERAL visited the Bn & inspected No ~~No~~ 3 & 4 Coy at drill &c. No 1 & 2 Coy were on the Range, musketry.	

D. D. & L., London, E.C. (A8 04) Wt W1771/M2031 750,000 5/17 Sch. 52 Forms/C2118/14

Instructions regarding War Diaries and Intelligence Summaries are contained in F. S. Regs., Part II. and the Staff Manual respectively. Title pages will be prepared in manuscript.

WAR DIARY
or
INTELLIGENCE SUMMARY.
(Erase heading not required.)

Army Form C. 2118.

2nd Battn IRISH GUARDS.

Place	Date 1918.	Hour	Summary of Events and Information	Remarks and references to Appendices
VILLERS-BRULIN.	MARCH. 14th		The MAJOR-GENERAL again visited the Bn & inspected No 1 & 2 Coys at drill. No 3 & 4 Coys also doing steady drill. Too wet for the range.- Lecture by the C.O. to Officers & N.C.O's on lessons learnt in the last tour in the line.	
	15th		No 3 & 4 Coys on the range. No 1 & 2 steady drill & inspections. The C.O. left to take temporary command of the Brigade. MAJOR LONG-INNES taking over the Bn.	
	16th		Route march.	
	17th		St. Patricks day. Battn parade for Mass in morning. A good dinner was prepared for the Bn who were visited by the MAJOR-GENERAL at their dinner. Shamrock was presented to the Bn before Mass. In the afternoon the Div. Cross Country Race was run the 4/Brigadier (the Comdg Officer) coming in a very easy first. The Bn team coming in 3rd.	
	18th		Coys under Coy Comdrs for drill inspections &c. The C.O. returned to the Battn.	
	19th		The officers & N.C.O's proceeded by lorry to a demonstration of the Cooperation of Tanks & Infantry. The remainder of the Bn doing arm drill &c under the Sergt Major.-	
	20th		Drill attack practised in morning.-	
	21st		Brigade Field Day - & conference with Brigadier afterwards. In afternoon finals of the Divisional Sports. Tug of war & Boxing. The Bn was beaten in the tug of war 2 pulls to 1, by 15th W. YORKS REGT, but won the middle & welter weights being 1st & 2nd in each.	

D. D. & L., London, E.C. (A8·04) Wt W1771/M2031 750,000 5/17 Sch. 52 Forms/C2118/14

Instructions regarding War Diaries and Intelligence Summaries are contained in F. S. Regs., Part II. and the Staff Manual respectively. Title pages will be prepared in manuscript.

WAR DIARY 2nd Bn Irish Guards

~~or~~

~~INTELLIGENCE SUMMARY.~~

(*Erase heading not required.*)

Army Form C. 2118.

4

Place	Date	Hour	Summary of Events and Information	Remarks and references to Appendices
VILLERS BRULIN	March 22nd	1am	Warning order received that Bde would probably move by bus at 8 a.m.	
		7.15am	Order to move received. The Battalion was on the road by 8.30am and marched via BETHENCOURT and TINCQUES to the embussing point on the ARRAS – St POL road.	
		10am	The convoy started for the battle travelling through St POL – FREVENT to BEAUMETZ. Here C.O.s met the Brigadier at the head of the column and the situation was explained by the G.S.O. 1. The column then went forward again via	
		6pm	BRETENCOURT and debussed at X5b77. Packs were dumped here and extra S.A.A. etc issued.	
		11pm	A conference of C.O.s took place where they were informed that the 31st Division was to go through into the line and were to hold the ground W of St LEGER. The 4th GUARDS to hold from BANK COPSE to a point 1000x S of Sensee river. The 2nd Bn Irish Guards (right) from BANK COPSE to Sensee river. Each Bn to have two Coys in front line and two in support.	
		11.30pm	The column started off marching via HAMELINCOURT took up the position in the Army line which had already been dug to a depth of 3 ft.	

D. D. & L., London, E.C.
(A8 04) Wt W1771/M2031 750,000 5/17 Sch 52 Forms/C2118/14

5

WAR DIARY *2nd Bn Irish Guards*
or
INTELLIGENCE SUMMARY.
(Erase heading not required.)

Army Form C. 2118.

Instructions regarding War Diaries and Intelligence Summaries are contained in F. S. Regs., Part II. and the Staff Manual respectively. Title pages will be prepared in manuscript.

Place	Date	Hour	Summary of Events and Information	Remarks and references to Appendices
	March 23rd		Dispositions were now as follows: No 3 Coy (left) No 1 Coy (right) from SENSEE river [illegible] in [illegible] line. No 2 Coy (right) No 4 Coy (left) in [illegible] line from ARRAS – ALBERT road to the SENSEE river. Bn H.Q. in Sunken road at B 1 b 2.8. There was heavy shelling of our front line during the day. In the evening it was arranged that the 4th GUARDS BDE should [illegible] + hold the ground S of the SENSEE river. Owing to the lateness of the relief this could not be completed so the 2 Coys of Irish Guards were withdrawn	
	24th		to the [illegible] line near Bn H.Q. During the day there was again heavy shelling of the front line [illegible] of the river + in the morning the Germans attacked but were driven off leaving several dead [illegible]. It was then arranged that 2nd Bn Irish Guards should move to right of [illegible] i.e. from B [illegible] 5.9 to B 9 d 8.0 and to relieve 13th Bn YORKSHIRE [illegible] and 21st Bn MIDDLESEX [illegible].	

D. D. & L., London, E.C.
(A8-04) Wt W1771/M2031 750,000 5/17 Sch. 52 Forms/C2118/14

6.

Instructions regarding War Diaries and Intelligence Summaries are contained in F. S. Regs., Part II. and the Staff Manual respectively. Title pages will be prepared in manuscript.

WAR DIARY *or* INTELLIGENCE SUMMARY.

2nd Bn Irish Guards

(*Erase heading not required.*)

Army Form C. 2118.

Place	Date	Hour	Summary of Events and Information	Remarks and references to Appendices
ERVILLERS AREA	24th	9pm.	Coys marched off to take up new position. Dispositions: No 2 right No 1 (centre) No 4 (left). No 3 support 400x in rear of No 3. Grenadiers in same position on left and COLDSTREAM GDS in reserve at B.8.A + D. with R. flank facing MORY.	
		10pm	Bn. H.Q + No 3 Coy had just reached their new Headquarters at B.8.C.6.3. when rifle fire was heard from direction of MORY. Soon followed by men streaming down the road past ~~Bn H~~ Q. They brought news that the enemy had broken through at MORY COPSE + were advancing on ERVILLERS. Enemy Very lights could now be seen from B.15.c. The right flank of the Bn was now entirely exposed. To meet this situation No 3 Coy who had not yet reached their destination was ordered to line the road from Bn H.Q to ERVILLERS. Here they came under heavy rifle + M.G. fire from high ground E of ERVILLERS. The remnants of YORKS and MANCHESTERS were collected together with stray Bn H.Q etc and were made to line the road from Bn H.Q N.E.	

A8091) Wt. W1 71/M2031 750,000 5/17 Sch. 52 Forms/C2118/14 D. D. & L., London, E.C.

Instructions regarding War Diaries and Intelligence Summaries are contained in F. S. Regs., Part II. and the Staff Manual respectively. Title pages will be prepared in manuscript.

WAR DIARY 2nd Bn Irish Guards.
or
INTELLIGENCE SUMMARY.
(*Erase heading not required.*)

Army Form C. 2118.

7

Place	Date	Hour	Summary of Events and Information	Remarks and references to Appendices
ERVILLERS AREA	24th	12 m.n.	No 1 + 2 Coy were ordered to swing back & to form a defensive flank to the South. The men lining the road were moved forward to join up with No 2 Coy.	
	25th	12:30 am	By 12:30 a.m. the defensive flank was continuous & in process of being dug from the original front-line down to ERVILLERS.	
			Soon after this No 3 Coy relieved the unit on the right of No 2 Coy so the whole Bn was now together. There was some shelling at intervals during the day. The enemy could be seen advancing into the valley between BEHAGNIES + ERVILLERS.	2Lt DALTON I/c of No 4 Coy was wounded
			In the evening Bn H.Q. & the SENSEE valley were heavily shelled by a battery of our 6" howitzers.	Capt Hon. H. O. O'BRIEN 2 in C wounded
		7pm.	Orders were received for the withdrawal to commence at 9 p.m.	
			Coys concentrated at Bn H.Q. and leaving 1 Platoon as rear guard marched off across country to take up a position on the high ground from COURCELLES to MOYENVILLE.	

D. D. & L., London, E.C. (A8001) Wt. W1 71/M2031 750,000 5/17 Sch. 52 Forms/C2118/14

Instructions regarding War Diaries and Intelligence Summaries are contained in F. S. Regs., Part II. and the Staff Manual respectively. Title pages will be prepared in manuscript.

WAR DIARY
or
INTELLIGENCE SUMMARY.
(Erase heading not required.)

2nd Bn Irish Guards

Army Form C. 2118.

8

Place	Date	Hour	Summary of Events and Information	Remarks and references to Appendices
COURCELLES ridge	25th	11 pm	Total frontage of the Bde was 3000x. 3rd Bn COLDSTREAM GDS (right) 2nd Bn IRISH GDS (centre), 4th Bn GRENADIER GDS (left). Trenches were sighted by the Commanding Officer [illegible] Offrs & Coys began to dig in at about 12 m.n. The Bn held from A9 b5 9 to A8 d 8.1 & was disposed from right to left No 1, 2, 3 No 4 Coy. Each with three platoons in front line & 1 platoon in support.	
	26th	5 am	Orders were recd to move at once to AYETTE where 4th GUARDS BDE would come into reserve. The 92nd & 93rd Bdes were to occupy the line which had just been dug.	
			New dispositions as follows: 2nd Bn Irish Guards (left) in Spur N.E. of AYETTE, 3rd Bn COLDSTREAM GUARDS in Spur S.W. of AYETTE, 4th Bn GRENADIER GUARDS in reserve (see map). The Bn was now in touch with the GUARDS DIVISION on left at S.1 b 2.8.	

D. D. & L., London, E.C. (A8001) Wt. W1 71/M2031 750,000 5/17 Sch. 52 Forms/C2118/14

Army Form C. 2118.

Instructions regarding War Diaries and Intelligence Summaries are contained in F. S. Regs., Part II. and the Staff Manual respectively. Title pages will be prepared in manuscript.

WAR DIARY
or
INTELLIGENCE SUMMARY.
(Erase heading not required.)

2nd Bn Irish Guards

Place	Date	Hour	Summary of Events and Information	Remarks and references to Appendices
AYETTE	26th		It was arranged that the Bn should be responsible for	
			the defence of AYETTE & No 1 Coy were sent to dig in on	
			S.W. end of the village. Owing to the length of the	
			Bn frontage (2000x) the line could not be held continuously	
			and the defence of the village itself was based largely	
			on cross M.G. fire from the high ground in rear.	
			During the afternoon owing to the enemy getting	
			into MOYENVILLE No 3 Coy were sent up to dig in	
			W of the village & fill up the gap in our defensive	
			line. During this operation they came under heavy	
	8pm		M.G. fire and lost 1 officer & 16 O.R. At 8 pm	
			the Coy was relieved & rejoined the Bn.	
	27th		At about 11 am the enemy put down an exceedingly	
			heavy barrage on 92nd & 93rd Bdes and at midday	
			attacked these two Bdes who were afterwards forced	

D. D. & L., London, E.C.
(A8001) Wt. W1 71/M2031 750,000 5/17 Sch. 52 Forms/C2118/14

10.

Instructions regarding War Diaries and Intelligence Summaries are contained in F. S. Regs., Part II. and the Staff Manual respectively. Title pages will be prepared in manuscript.

WAR DIARY
or
INTELLIGENCE SUMMARY.
(Erase heading not required.)

2nd Bn Irish Guards

Army Form C. 2118.

Place	Date	Hour	Summary of Events and Information	Remarks and references to Appendices
AYETTE	27th		leaving the 4th GUARDS BDE once more in the front line. The enemy advanced no further than the old aerodrome W A D C	
			Our line was at this point reinforced by 2 Coys Grenadier Guards and 100 E. LANCS	
		10am	The Commanding Officer was sent for to take command of the Bde owing to Brigadier General Lord ARDEE being forced to go sick from the effects of gas poisoning.	
			Major P S LONG-INNES arrived at 12 m.n. & took over command of the Bn.	
	28th		Except for a little shelling the day passed quietly. Our posts were withdrawn from in front of AYETTE and the 3rd Bn C. G. moved forward to take up the line of the BUCQUOY - AYETTE road	

D. D. & L., London, E.C. (A5003) Wt. W1 71/M2031 750,000 5/17 Sch. 52 Forms/C2118/14

WAR DIARY
or
INTELLIGENCE SUMMARY.
(*Erase heading not required.*)

2nd Bn [illegible]

Army Form C. 2118.

11

Instructions regarding War Diaries and Intelligence Summaries are contained in F. S. Regs., Part II. and the Staff Manual respectively. Title pages will be prepared in manuscript.

Place	Date	Hour	Summary of Events and Information	Remarks and references to Appendices
AYETTE	29th		Snipers in AYETTE became active but otherwise the day passed quietly.	[illegible]
	30th		Snipers became increasingly active and rendered movement in our line almost impossible. To cope with this our 4.5 Howitzers fired on the village for 15 min and did much to improve the situation.	
		10pm	A German sniper walked into our lines and was captured. He belonged to 466th Regt.	
	31st	[illegible]	15 mins intense barrage was put down on the village	
		9pm	The Battalion was relieved by 2nd Bn MANCHESTER Regt & marched out to billets at BIENVILLERS.	

D. D. & L., London, E.C.
(A8031) Wt. W1 71/M2031 750,000 5/17 Sch. 52 Forms/C2118/14

4th Guards Brigade.

31st Division.

- -------------

2nd BATTALION

THE IRISH GUARDS

APRIL 1918.

Instructions regarding War Diaries and Intelligence Summaries are contained in F. S. Regs., Part II. and the Staff Manual respectively. Title pages will be prepared in manuscript.

WAR DIARY
or
INTELLIGENCE SUMMARY.
(Erase heading not required.)

Army Form C. 2118.

34

2nd Bn IRISH GUARDS

Place	Date April	Hour	Summary of Events and Information	Remarks and references to Appendices
BIENVILLERS to SOMBRIN	1918. 1st		The Battn marched from BIENVILLERS to SOMBRIN, arriving 7.30 p.m.	
SOMBRIN to CHELERS	2nd		The Battn marched from SOMBRIN to LIENCOURT where they embussed & proceeded to TINCQUETTE where they de-bussed & marched into billets at CHELERS.	
CHELERS	3rd		The day spent in Coy. Inspections cleaning up billets &c.	
	4th		Coy. Inspections & steady drill. The Comdg Officer returned to the Battn. A draft of 224 O.R. arrived with Lt BULLER (who subsequently proceeded to join 1st Battn) & 2/Lt KENT.	
	5th		The new draft was inspected by the Comdg Officer. Coys at the disposal of Coy. Comdrs for drill & musketry. CAPT. MOORE & Lt KEENAN arrived - the former posted to No 1 Coy temporarily pending taking over duties as 2nd in Comd. the latter attached to B.H.Q. as Sniping Bombing & Intelligence Officer.	

A5834 Wt. W4973/M687 750,000 8/16 D. D. & L. Ltd. Forms/C.2118/13

Instructions regarding War Diaries and Intelligence Summaries are contained in F. S. Regs., Part II. and the Staff Manual respectively. Title pages will be prepared in manuscript.

(2) Army Form C. 2118.

WAR DIARY
or
~~INTELLIGENCE SUMMARY.~~
(Erase heading not required.)

2nd BATTn IRISH GUARDS.

Place	APRIL Date 1918.	Hour	Summary of Events and Information	Remarks and references to Appendices
CHELERS.	6th		Lecture, followed by demonstration by Cmd Officer to all Officers & N.C.Os on "Lessons learnt in the recent Operations", "Advance Guards", "Patrols" etc. — Coys practising these movements afterwards. A draft of 62 O.R. arrived & were inspected by the Cmd Officer. In the afternoon the DRUMS attended a CORPS BAND & DRUM competition at BRYAS. The DRUMS were awarded 11th place out of 35.	
	7th		Church Parade & Baths.	
	8th		Battn Parade & Coy. training.	
	9th		~~Batt~~ BRIGADE Parade to practise Ceremonial for MAJOR-GENERAL'S Inspection.	
	10th		The 4th GUARDS BRIGADE was inspected by the MAJOR GENERAL, who afterwards addressed the Brigade & complimented them on the fine work they had done in the recent Operations. Orders were received at mid-day for the Battn to proceed to unknown destination forthwith. The Bn marched out at 10.30 p.m. to the ARRAS-TINCQUES road where they were to embus at 11.30 p.m. The buses [illegible] however & the night was spent by the roadside.	

A5834 Wt. W4973/M687 750,000 8/16 D. D. & L. Ltd. Forms/C.2118/13.

Instructions regarding War Diaries and Intelligence Summaries are contained in F. S. Regs., Part II. and the Staff Manual respectively. Title pages will be prepared in manuscript.

WAR DIARY
or
~~INTELLIGENCE SUMMARY.~~
(*Erase heading not required.*)

Army Form C. 2118.

2nd Bn Irish Guards.

Place	Date 1918	Hour	Summary of Events and Information	Remarks and references to Appendices
	April 11th		Busses arrived about 8 am. The Brigade embussed and proceeded to STRAZEELE via St POL — FREVENT — St VENANT — FORET of [illegible] — HAZEBROUCK.	
			From 9 pm 11th April — 14th April see Narrative.	
	April 15th		The Bn was billeted in small Farms 1000 yds South of BORRE. At 6 pm the Brigadier held a conference of Commanding Officers at Bde HQ and discussed the question of fighting strength. Owing to the heaviness of casualties suffered by the Brigade, it was decided to form the 4th Bn Grenadier Guards and 3rd Bn Coldstream Guards each into 2 companies, and for tactical purposes to make these into 1 Bn under the senior CO. The KOYLI 12th Bn (Pioneers) were brought into the Brigade as a fighting unit.	

A5834 Wt. W4973/M687 750,000 8/16 D. D. & L. Ltd. Forms/C.2118/13

Instructions regarding War Diaries and Intelligence Summaries are contained in F. S. Regs., Part II. and the Staff Manual respectively. Title pages will be prepared in manuscript.

WAR DIARY
or
~~INTELLIGENCE SUMMARY.~~

(*Erase heading not required.*)

2nd Bn Irish Guards

Army Form C. 2118.

Place	Date	Hour	Summary of Events and Information	Remarks and references to Appendices
	April 16th		During the morning the CO, 2nd in C and 4 company commanders went [illegible] to inspect a rear line behind [illegible]. The Bn were shelled in billets and to prevent casualties were moved into the fields and made to dig in, in little trenches. Captain C [illegible] Moore [illegible] whilst riding round the [illegible] with the CO was hit by a piece of shell, actually at the moment of dismounting. No other casualties in spite of shells dropping everywhere.	
	April 17th		Moved at 5 pm towards the line to take the place of the 3rd Australian Brigade in Reserve. The companies were billeted in Grand Marquette [illegible] and La [illegible]. Bn HQ in D.6.c.8.5. The orders were to man the reserve line in the event of stand to. By day the Bn were to work on improving the reserve line. [illegible] in touch with the 11th [illegible] on our left and 12th Bn [illegible] on the right. The Grenadiers and Coldstream being in reserve.	

A5834 Wt. W4973/M687 750,000 8/16 D. D. & L. Ltd. Forms/C.2118/13

Instructions regarding War Diaries and Intelligence Summaries are contained in F. S. Regs., Part II. and the Staff Manual respectively. Title pages will be prepared in manuscript.

WAR DIARY

or

~~INTELLIGENCE SUMMARY.~~

(Erase heading not required.)

Army Form C. 2118.

(5)

2nd Bn Irish Guards

Place	Date	Hour	Summary of Events and Information	Remarks and references to Appendices
	April 18th		Work was carried out in the line — Coys digging all day	
			No 2 & 4 Coy commanders visited the front line that night [illegible]	
	April 19th		No 1 and 3 Coys relieved 2 coys of the Australians about 2 pm in the support line in the Bois D'Avel. Bn HQ and No 2 & 4 Coys marched off about 6 pm, given guides at the entrance to the forest and marched into the line. The Bn was disposed as follows No 1 Coy right — No 2 Coy left each with 2 platoon posts in the front line and 1 platoon in support. No 4 Coy support and No 3 Coy reserve, stretched out in a line of posts, through the wood. Bn HQ near the Saw Mill at [illegible]. Relief was complete about 10 pm.	
			The 12th Bn [illegible] who were on our right shared the Bn HQ with us	

A5834 Wt. W4973/M687 750,000 8/16 D. D. & L. Ltd. Forms/C.2118/13

WAR DIARY
or
INTELLIGENCE SUMMARY.
(Erase heading not required.)

Army Form C. 2118.

Instructions regarding War Diaries and Intelligence Summaries are contained in F. S. Regs., Part II. and the Staff Manual respectively. Title pages will be prepared in manuscript.

Place	Date	Hour	Summary of Events and Information	Remarks and references to Appendices
Line	April 20th		The line was exceptionally quiet, our front line posts were well hidden behind hedges and the men were not allowed to show themselves or light fires, so it is probable the enemy did not know our exact positions. The nearest Germany posts were [illegible], but they no doubt assumed the same tactics as ourselves, with the result that we were unable to locate their trenches.	
	April 21st		The day was quiet except round Bn. HQ. where, from 4 to 8 pm the Bosche shelled with 8 in, but these were aimed for the road and Bridge, and luckily none of their shells actually fell into HQ although many were unpleasantly near. At 10.15 pm the Germans threw over many gas shells — so bad was the gassing that Bn HQ were obliged to move into the wood — to the South. The shelling continued till 2 am, and caused rather a number of casualties. The gas fumes hanging in the thick undergrowth for considerable time. No 1 & 3 coy relieved No 2 & 4 coy in the front line during the night	

A5834 Wt. W4973/M687 750,000 8/16 D. D. & L. Ltd. Forms/C.2118/13

Instructions regarding War Diaries and Intelligence Summaries are contained in F. S. Regs., Part II. and the Staff Manual respectively. Title pages will be prepared in manuscript.

WAR DIARY
or
~~INTELLIGENCE SUMMARY.~~
(*Erase heading not required.*)

Army Form C. 2118.

(9)

2nd Bn Irish Guards

Place	Date	Hour	Summary of Events and Information	Remarks and references to Appendices
Line	April 22nd		Nothing of interest during the day. No 1 company was right front coy and No 3 coy left front coy. No 2 coy moved up on the left of No 4 coy, so the support line was continuous. Work was done on this line and consisted of a chain of posts, well wired. The wood was so swampy that posts had to be built up, water being reached about 2 feet under the surface of the ground. The enemy again gassed heavily from 2 am – 6 am on the night of the 22nd/23rd. Sgt. Bellew with a patrol of 2 others left our lines to gain identification. He brought back a prisoner from a listening post about 100 metres S.W. of Fm BEAULIEU. It is of interest that the prisoner who belonged to the 221 Regt (48 DIV) was put into the ERSATZ because he was deaf and was as stated above captured in a listening post!!	

A5834 Wt. W4973/M687 750,000 8/16 D. D. & L. Ltd. Forms/C.2118/13

Instructions regarding War Diaries and Intelligence Summaries are contained in F. S. Regs., Part II. and the Staff Manual respectively. Title pages will be prepared in manuscript.

WAR DIARY
or
~~INTELLIGENCE SUMMARY~~.
(Erase heading not required.)

Army Form C. 2118.

(8)

2nd Bn Irish Guards

Place	Date	Hour	Summary of Events and Information	Remarks and references to Appendices
Line.	April 23rd		The day passed quietly. During the afternoon No 2 & 4 coys were relieved in the support line by a company of the 12th Bn KOYLI (D coy). No 2 & 4 coys only numbered 80 men, and these were formed into the raiding party, under Lt MATHEW and 2nd Lt O'CLOSE. The party were detailed into sections and practiced over a laid out course in the wood, during the afternoon. For the raid see Narrative. The raid on BEAULIEU Fm was entirely successful, thanks to our careful preparation — the excellence of the artillery & machine gun barrage and above all to the incomparable dash of our troops. We captured 25 prisoners — one of whom could speak English fluently having been a steward on the Nord Deutscher Lloyd in peace time. He was a well educated man and his views on the war and the general situation were interesting. He owned to the food shortage in Germany and said that his country were determined to finish the war this summer. They had large reserves of men, who had been training all winter.	

A5834 Wt. W4973/M687 750,000 8/16 D. D. & L. Ltd. Forms/C.2118/13

Army Form C. 2118.

Instructions regarding War Diaries and Intelligence Summaries are contained in F. S. Regs., Part II. and the Staff Manual respectively. Title pages will be prepared in manuscript.

WAR DIARY
or
~~INTELLIGENCE SUMMARY.~~

(*Erase heading not required.*)

(9)

2nd Bn. Irish Guards.

Place	Date	Hour	Summary of Events and Information	Remarks and references to Appendices
Line	April 23rd		All the prisoners who could speak English, confessed they were all very sick and tired of the war and undoubtedly by their behaviour they were delighted at being taken prisoner. What was very noticeable, was their excellent discipline ~~as here~~ as captives not a man failed to spring smartly to attention when spoken to by an officer. It is undoubtedly this iron discipline which has made success possible for them.	
	April 24th		The day passed quietly and in the evening No 1 and 3 Coys were relieved by the 3rd Bn. Coldstream Guards. On completion of the relief Coys marched back to billets round LE TIR ANGLAIS where the Bn. came into support. The Commanding Officer took over command of the Brigade, owing to the Brigadier going sick owing to gas poisoning.	
	April 25th } 26th }		There is nothing of interest to report — the Bn. found small parties to work on the reserve line, otherwise the men spent the days in cleaning and resting. On the 25th a draft of 59 O.R. arrived from Home	

Instructions regarding War Diaries and Intelligence Summaries are contained in F. S. Regs., Part II. and the Staff Manual respectively. Title pages will be prepared in manuscript.

WAR DIARY
or
~~INTELLIGENCE SUMMARY.~~
(Erase heading not required.)

Army Form C. 2118.

(10)

2nd Bn Irish Guards

Place	Date	Hour	Summary of Events and Information	Remarks and references to Appendices
	April 27th		During the day the Bn was relieved by 2 coys of the Royal Dublin Fusiliers and 2 coys of the Lancashire Fusiliers. About 6 pm the Bn marched off to HONDINGHAM where billets were arranged for the Brigade. The CO returned to the Bn taking over from Captain T. Nugent.	
	April 28th		The coys were distributed in Fms near the town. Bn Hq being in a house near the Church. Father Browne held mass in the morning. Captain A.F.L. Gordon MC arrived from the 1st Bn to take over the duties of 2nd in command. Capt. H. Law also arrived from England.	
	April 29th		The morning was spent in thorough kit inspection & cleaning up parades etc.	
	April 30th		The whole Bn proceeded on fatigue & work on the LAMOTTE defences returning about 4 pm. Major Long-Innes MC proceeded to England on duty.	

H.R. Alexander Lt Col
Commanding 2nd Bn Irish Guards

A5834 Wt. W4973/M687 750,000 8/16 D. D. & L. Ltd. Forms/C.2118/13

WAR DIARY
or
INTELLIGENCE ~~SUMMARY~~.
(Erase heading not required.)

Army Form C. 2118.

Instructions regarding War Diaries and Intelligence Summaries are contained in F. S. Regs., Part II. and the Staff Manual respectively. Title pages will be prepared in manuscript.

May, 1918
2nd Bn Irish Guards. (1)
Vol 35

Place	Date	Hour	Summary of Events and Information	Remarks and references to Appendices
HONDEGHEM	~~APRIL~~ MAY 1st	1918	200 O.R. under 4 Officers were detailed to work on the HAZEBROUCK defences in V.30. Working parties were to commence at 9 am and to cease work at 1 pm. These parties proceeded in fighting order and took haversack rations with them. 20 O.R. per coy were left behind to be instructed in Lewis Gunnery.	
	2nd	"	Usual routine. Companies were put under orders of their company commanders for training in open warfare movements. During the afternoon companies paraded for inspection of box respirators and anti-gas drill. The remaining officers of the Bn paraded under an officer instructor of the XV Corps and carried out a simple tactical scheme during the morning.	
	3rd	"	200 O.R. (about 50 men per company) under their respective officers were detailed to work on the HAZEBROUCK Defences at V.30. The work consisted in digging or rather building up parapets along a continuous line in the required area. The country is so low in this part of Flanders that it is impossible to dig more than a foot below the surface without striking water. Baths in the afternoon.	

A5834 Wt. W4973/M687 750,000 8/16 D. D. & L. Ltd. Forms/C.2118/13

Army Form C. 2118.

WAR DIARY
or
INTELLIGENCE SUMMARY.
(Erase heading not required.)

2nd Bn Irish Guards (2)

Instructions regarding War Diaries and Intelligence Summaries are contained in F. S. Regs., Part II. and the Staff Manual respectively. Title pages will be prepared in manuscript.

Place	Date	Hour	Summary of Events and Information	Remarks and references to Appendices
HONDEGHEM.	~~APRIL~~ MAY 4th	1918	The usual working party of 200 O.R. worked in V.30. Baths were allotted to those who could not be bathed on the previous day. In the evening at 7.15 the massed drums of the Brigade and pipers of the Bn played in the Square of the town. This was a most impressive spectacle and was much appreciated by the inhabitants and the neighbouring troops.	
"	5th	"	Sunday. R.C. paraded and held mass in the Church of HONDEGHEM. C of E parties paraded and service was held in the field of No 4 company's billet.	
"	6th	"	The same numbers were required for digging in V.30 but as usual the L.G. [illegible] and signallers were excused their work in order to be instructed in their respective branches as specialists. The following names of Officers and O.R. appeared as receiving Honours and Awards: Captain J. LAWSON (R.A.M.C.) — M.C. " " Hon H.B. O'BRIEN — M.C. Lt. R. HEARD — M.C. Lt. F.S. SMITH — M.C. 2nd Lt. J.A.S. GATTI — M.C. No 2506 Sgt T. REILLY M.M. — D.C.M. No 5823 Sgt T. MURRAY — D.C.M.	

A5834 Wt. W4973/M687 750,000 8/16 D. D. & L. Ltd. Forms/C.2118/13

Army Form C. 2118.

Instructions regarding War Diaries and Intelligence Summaries are contained in F. S. Regs., Part II. and the Staff Manual respectively. Title pages will be prepared in manuscript.

WAR DIARY
or
INTELLIGENCE SUMMARY.
(Erase heading not required.)

2nd Bn Irish Guards (3)

Place	Date	Hour	Summary of Events and Information	Remarks and references to Appendices
HONDEGHEM	MAY ~~APRIL~~ 7th	1918	The Bn supplied 200 men to work on the HAZEBROUCK Defences in V 30. Work commencing at 9 am.	
"	8th	"	Bn parade at 9 am. Lewis gunners and Signallers as usual paraded separately under their respective instructors. The massed drums of the Brigade and the pipes played in the square of the town at Tattoo.	
	9th	"	All Officers and NCOs paraded at 9 am for a lecture and demonstration by the C.O. on the methods applied by the Germans in attacking across open country, and the means necessary to combat their tactics. From 10.30 am – 12 noon companies were placed at the disposal of their officers to lecture and instruct in the lesson taught by the Commanding Officer the previous hour.	

A5834 Wt. W4973/M687 750,000 8/16 D. D. & L. Ltd. Forms/C.2118/13

Instructions regarding War Diaries and Intelligence Summaries are contained in F. S. Regs., Part II. and the Staff Manual respectively. Title pages will be prepared in manuscript.

WAR DIARY
or
INTELLIGENCE SUMMARY.
(Erase heading not required.)

2nd Bn Irish Guards

Army Form C. 2118.

(4)

Place	Date	Hour	Summary of Events and Information	Remarks and references to Appendices
HONDEGHEM	MAY ~~April~~ 10th	1918	170 O.R. were found by the Bn for digging — the scenes of their activities were displayed in the neighbourhood of CAESTRE which is farther than V.30, but here the country is more hilly and it is possible to dig without coming to water. The lines in this area were only dug to a depth of 2 ft. — spit locked.	
			The undermentioned Officers appeared in the honours list.	
			Capt. G.L. Bainbridge } Military Cross.	
			" C.J. O'H Moore }	
			" T.P.G. Nugent }	
			L/Cpl. T. Coard } M.M.	
			Pte J. Gault }	
			" R. Gardner }	
			" J. O'Flaherty }	
			L/Sgt. C. Baker }	M.M
			Pte H. Neale (attached) }	
			Most of the O.R. were awarded for the successful raid (a raid) on the lines on BEAULIEU Fm on April 23rd	
			Pte Neale was the young soldier belonging to the 1st Bn D.C.L.I. who attached himself to the Bn when he lost his own during the fighting near the HAZEBROUCK Rd and who so gallantly went over with the raiding party.	

A5834 Wt. W4973/M687 750,000 8/16 D. D. & L. Ltd. Forms/C.2118/13

Instructions regarding War Diaries and Intelligence Summaries are contained in F. S. Regs., Part II. and the Staff Manual respectively. Title pages will be prepared in manuscript.

WAR DIARY
or
~~INTELLIGENCE SUMMARY.~~
(Erase heading not required.)

Army Form C. 2118.

2nd Bn Irish Guards (5)

Place	Date	Hour	Summary of Events and Information	Remarks and references to Appendices
HONEGHEM	MAY 11th	1916	A party of 150 O.R were detailed for working on the trenches around CAESTRE.	
"	12th	"	The usual Church parades. At 11.30 am the Brigadier inspected the transport lines and appeared very pleased with the excellent condition of the horses and the general appearance of the transport.	
"	13th	"	200 O.R were found for the usual work near CAESTRE. At [illegible] the massed drums and pipes played in the town.	
"	14th	"	During the morning the Brigade paraded in the aerodrome in P. 31. a and carried out a rehearsal for the inspection of the Brigade by the Commander of the 2nd Army. The parade was carried out without any hitch, but the drill was bad and the men dispirited. (As is always often the case with these rehearsals.) Baths were allotted to the Bn in the afternoon.	

A5834 Wt. W4973/M687 750,000 8/16 D. D. & L. Ltd. Forms/C.2118/13

Instructions regarding War Diaries and Intelligence Summaries are contained in F. S. Regs., Part II. and the Staff Manual respectively. Title pages will be prepared in manuscript.

WAR DIARY
or
INTELLIGENCE SUMMARY.
(Erase heading not required.)

Army Form C. 2118.

2nd Bn Irish Guards (6)

Place	Date	Hour	Summary of Events and Information	Remarks and references to Appendices
HONDEGHEM.	MAY. 15th	1918	The Bn was organised into 2 companies each of 55 file. This was done owing to the shortage in numbers. Dress drill order without pouches. Men to receive medals paraded in walking out order without rifles but with bayonets. Officers did not carry sticks – only mounted Officers (C.O. 2nd in C. Adjt) wore gloves. The Bn paraded at 10.30 am and was to be in position at 12 noon. The Army Commander (General Plumer) inspected each Bn and personally complimented the CO on the turn out, style and magnificence of the men. This remark was thoroughly deserved. The Bn looked well, very well and the general was much struck with the number of men who had been wounded. Medal ribbons were presented, Commanding Officer relating ~~a small~~ a short account of each deed which had earned an award. This was followed by the march past. The Army Commander then made a very nice address to the Brigade. The parade was an undoubted success the turn out and drill being excellent.	

A5834 Wt. W4973/M687 750,000 8/16 D. D. & L. Ltd. Forms/C.2118/13

Instructions regarding War Diaries and Intelligence Summaries are contained in F. S. Regs., Part II. and the Staff Manual respectively. Title pages will be prepared in manuscript.

WAR DIARY
or
~~INTELLIGENCE SUMMARY.~~
(Erase heading not required.)

Army Form C. 2118.

2nd Bn Irish Guards (7)

Place	Date	Hour	Summary of Events and Information	Remarks and references to Appendices
HONDEGHEM	MAY 16th	1918	200 O.R. were found for work on rear lines near CAESTRE. The usual routine during the morning.	
" "	17th	"	During the morning companies were placed at the disposal of their company commanders.	
" "	18th	"	The same programme as for the 17th.	
" "	19th	"	180 O.R. detailed to work near CAESTRE. The usual specialists paraded under their instructors for instruction. In the list of Honours and awards the following names appeared: 2nd Lt T. MATHEW — Military Cross } for the raid on April 23rd; No 2050 Sgt R. WARSH — D.C.M.	
			During the whole of our stay at HONDEGHEM the Bn was in Corps Reserve and at 1 hours notice, except for the last few days. The weather was very fine and the Bn played cricket most afternoons. Little training could be carried out except for training a few specialists owing to the number required for digging.	

A5834 Wt. W4973/M687 750,000 8/16 D. D. & L. Ltd. Forms/C.2118/13

Instructions regarding War Diaries and Intelligence Summaries are contained in F. S. Regs., Part II. and the Staff Manual respectively. Title pages will be prepared in manuscript.

WAR DIARY
or
~~INTELLIGENCE SUMMARY.~~ 2nd Bn Irish Guards

(Erase heading not required.)

Army Form C. 2118.

(8)

Place	Date	Hour	Summary of Events and Information	Remarks and references to Appendices
From HONDEGHEM — BARLY WOOD	MAY 20th	1918	Bn paraded at 7.25 am in full marching order and proceeded by march route to the embussing point on the main St OMER HAZEBROUCK Rd at V.22.b.6.1. From this point the Bn bussed to St OMER station. Here we met the transport which had proceeded by road. The Bn entrained and got dinners at 12 noon. At 1 pm the train started. The day was very hot and the journey was very pleasant.	
			Train arrived in at MONDICOURT ST about 9 pm, where we were met by Lt Col J Alston ([illegible] Q.S. DW) and were provided with hot tea, chocolate and biscuits & cigarettes. This thoughtfulness was much appreciated. The drums of the 1st (first) Bn Grenadier Guards played us out of the station.	
			It was a long march but the Bn arrived into camp about	
	21st	"	1.30 am. The camp consists of tents in an open space in the middle of BARLY WOOD, with small huts for officers. 90 tents which means room for 7 or 8 men to a tent. A very comfortable billet in summer but unfortunately no water nearer than BARLY TOWN.	

A5834 Wt. W4973/M687 750,000 8/16 D. D. & L. Ltd. Forms/C.2118/13

Instructions regarding War Diaries and Intelligence Summaries are contained in F. S. Regs., Part II. and the Staff Manual respectively. Title pages will be prepared in manuscript.

WAR DIARY
or
INTELLIGENCE SUMMARY.
(Erase heading not required.)

2nd Bn Irish Guards

Army Form C. 2118.

Place	Date	Hour	Summary of Events and Information	Remarks and references to Appendices
BARLY CAMP. (P. 26.)	May 21st	1918	Reveille at 8 am The day was spent in improvement of the camp We received orders that in the event of an enemy attack penetrating our forward zone the roll of the Bn was to man the GHQ line which runs to the E of BARLY wood. This line is already dug.	
" "	22nd	"	Bn parade at 8 am for steady drill under the Adjutant Anti gas drill and lecture on the various forms of salutes etc at 10 am. Usual routine during the morning In the afternoon a suitable site was chosen in the camp for a cricket ground and a very good pitch was made	
"	23rd		Bn parade at 8 am – 9 am 10 am Officers paraded under the C.O. and reconnoitred the GHQ line	

A5834 Wt. W4973/M687 750,000 8/16 D. D. & L. Ltd. Forms/C.2118/13

Instructions regarding War Diaries and Intelligence Summaries are contained in F. S. Regs., Part II. and the Staff Manual respectively. Title pages will be prepared in manuscript.

WAR DIARY
or
~~INTELLIGENCE SUMMARY.~~

(Erase heading not required.)

2nd Bn Irish Guards (47)

Army Form C. 2118.

Place	Date	Hour	Summary of Events and Information	Remarks and references to Appendices
BARLY CAMP	MAY 24th	1918	Bn parade from 8 am – 9 am steady drill & saluting. From 10 am onwards the Bn took up the battle-positions and the C.O. proceeded round the line agreeing or altering the positions taken up by companies.	
"	25th	"	Bn parade from 8 am – 9 am. From 10 am – 12 noon companies were placed at the disposal of company commanders to practice march discipline etc. In the evening the C.O. rode over to the Brigade at GRENAS to spend the week end with the Brigadier.	
" "	26th		R.C. mass was held in the church at BARLY at 11 am. C of E service was held in camp at 12 noon.	

A5834 Wt. W4973/M687 750,000 8/16 D. D. & L. Ltd. Forms/C.2118/13

Army Form C. 2118.

Instructions regarding War Diaries and Intelligence Summaries are contained in F. S. Regs., Part II. and the Staff Manual respectively. Title pages will be prepared in manuscript.

WAR DIARY
or
~~INTELLIGENCE SUMMARY.~~

(Erase heading not required.)

2nd Bn Irish Guards.

Place	Date	Hour	Summary of Events and Information	Remarks and references to Appendices
BARRY CAMP	MAY 27th	1918	On Monday our new school of instruction opened. Owing to the small numbers of men and the few instructors, the Bn was divided into classes: those of the men being numbered from 1 – 13. about 20 in each class. Those for NCOs from A – D. 20 per class. No 1 coy being class 1, 2, 3, 4. No 2 coy class 5, 6 etc. NCOs classes were lettered, so that A class was made up of NCOs from No 1 coy and so on.	
			All the instructors in the following subjects were pooled & placed under an officer and the following subjects taught	
			1 Musketry under Major A Gordon M.C.	
			2 Tactics (only Officers & NCOs) under C.O.	
			3 L. G. under Lt W. D. Faulkner & Lt T. Brooke.	
			4 Bombing & Rifle grenade under Capt R. E. Sassoon M.C.	
			5 Map reading etc under Capt H. Law M.C. (Officers & NCOs only)	
			6. Drill under Adjutant.	
			In this way every officer NCO and man is being taught by competent instructors in the above subjects	

A5834 Wt. W4973/M687 750,000 8/16 D. D. & L. Ltd. Forms/C.2118/13

Army Form C. 2118.

Instructions regarding War Diaries and Intelligence Summaries are contained in F. S. Regs., Part II. and the Staff Manual respectively. Title pages will be prepared in manuscript.

WAR DIARY
or
INTELLIGENCE SUMMARY.
(Erase heading not required.)

2nd Bn Irish Guards (3) 7

Place	Date	Hour	Summary of Events and Information	Remarks and references to Appendices
BARLY CAMP	MAY 27 (cont)	1916	The following names appeared amongst those mentioned in despatches. Major A. F. L. Gordon M.C. Capt T. E. G. Nugent M.C. S.M. R. Gamble M.C.	
"	28th	"	Training as per programme. In addition to the usual programme of training the Bn parades every morning from 8 am – 9 am unless otherwise stated. Baths in BARLY during the morning for HQ drums and transport	
"	29th	"	Training as per programme and usual routine. The new school of instruction is a great success. NCOs and men are keen — individual attention can be given to each student because the classes are small and the work is varied so that a man does not get tired of one subject — a marked improvement is noticed in the drill of NCOs who are being taught	

A5834 Wt. W4973/M687 750,000 8/16 D. D. & L. Ltd. Forms/C.2118/13

Instructions regarding War Diaries and Intelligence Summaries are contained in F. S. Regs., Part II. and the Staff Manual respectively. Title pages will be prepared in manuscript.

WAR DIARY
or
INTELLIGENCE SUMMARY.
(Erase heading not required.)

2nd Bn Irish Guards. (14)

Army Form C. 2118.

Place	Date	Hour	Summary of Events and Information	Remarks and references to Appendices
BARLY	MAY 30th	1918	Training as per weekly programme. Brigadier inspected the new classes and was much impressed at the excellence of the training being carried out. Lts CLOSE, KENT, BURKE and DAGGER were sent to do duty with the 1st Bn	
	31st	"	Training as per weekly programme. From 10.30 am – 1 pm the Brigadier held a staff ride with Commanding Officers and their adjutants – when a small scheme was carried out	
General remarks			The weather for this month has been particularly fine and since being in BARLY CAMP cricket games & matches have been played every afternoon. This is a game which is gaining great popularity in the Bn. The only disadvantage is the lack of water but a shower bath is being erected for the men. Reveille has been at 6 am since our arrival in this camp.	
			B.R.C. " 6.45 am	
			Breakfast " 7 am Mon. 7.15 am	
			Sick parade " 7.30 am	
			Dinner " 12.30 pm	
			Ho? orders " 1.30 pm	
			CO orders " 1.45 pm	
				H. R. Alexander Lt Col Commanding 2nd Bn Irish Guards 1/6/18

A5834 Wt. W4973/M687 750,000 8/16 D. D. & L. Ltd. Forms/C.2118/13

40. On 8/2/18 4/G.G. 3/C.G.,
and 2/I.G. were formed into
4th Gds Bde (Br. Gen. Lord Ardee)
The Bde joined 31st Div at noon
on 8/2/18

On 12/2/18 94th M.G. Coy
and 94th T.M Bty joined the
Bde (temporarily)
The 4th Gds T.M. Bty was
formed on 16/3/18

Guards Division
4th Gds Bde.
2nd Bn Irish Gds.
June - Oct. 1918.

Instructions regarding War Diaries and Intelligence Summaries are contained in F. S. Regs., Part II. and the Staff Manual respectively. Title pages will be prepared in manuscript.

WAR DIARY
or
INTELLIGENCE ~~SUMMARY~~.
(Erase heading not required.)

June, 1918 ~~Army~~ Form C. 2118.

(1)

2nd Bn Irish Guards

Vol 36

Place	Date	Hour	Summary of Events and Information	Remarks and references to Appendices
BARLY CAMP.	JUNE 1918	1st	Training carried out according to programme as explained in the War Diary for last month.	
	"	2nd	Divine Service for R.Cs in SAULTY CHURCH at 9.30 am. C of E in Camp at 11.45 am. The CO inspected Camp after church. In the afternoon there was a Procession of the Blessed Sacrament at BARLY in which all the R.Cs of the Bn took part.	
	"	3rd	A working party of 100 OR under 2nd Lt E.H. DOWZER commenced digging a buried cable line at 5 am near WARLINCOURT HALT. Dress – fighting order. This task was completed at 8 am. Training as per programme. Pte F. TIMONEY ran 2nd in an open mile at SAULTY in the 4th Bn Grenadier Guards Sports.	
		4th	100 OR under 2nd Lt T MATHEW M.C. [illegible] work at WARLINCOURT HALT at 5 am. Training as per programme for remainder.	

A5834 Wt. W4973/M687 750,000 8/16 D. D. & L. Ltd. Forms/C.2118/13

Instructions regarding War Diaries and Intelligence Summaries are contained in F. S. Regs., Part II. and the Staff Manual respectively. Title pages will be prepared in manuscript.

WAR DIARY
or
~~INTELLIGENCE SUMMARY.~~

(Erase heading not required.)

2nd Bn Irish Guards

Army Form C. 2118.

(2)

Place	Date	Hour	Summary of Events and Information	Remarks and references to Appendices
BARLY CAMP	June 1918	5th	100 O.R. under 2nd Lt J BROOKS were detailed to hold themselves in readiness for work on the G.H.Q. line	
			Training as per programme.	
	" "	6th	60 O.R. worked under the AUSTRALIAN MINERS in the construction of dug-outs.	
			Training as per programme for the remainder of Bn	
			During the morning the Brigadier inspected the Camp and expressed his pleasure at the excellent appearance of everything.	
		7th	The required number (60 O.R.) detailed for work in dug out construction	
			Training as per programme.	
		8th	Work on mining and training as usual was carried out.	
		9th	Divine Service for R.Cs. in SAULTY CHURCH at 9.30 am. C of E in Camp at 10.45 am.	

A5834 Wt. W4973/M687 750,000 8/16 D. D. & L. Ltd. Forms/C.2118/13

Instructions regarding War Diaries and Intelligence Summaries are contained in F. S. Regs., Part II. and the Staff Manual respectively. Title pages will be prepared in manuscript.

WAR DIARY
or
~~INTELLIGENCE SUMMARY.~~ 2nd Bn Irish Guards.

(Erase heading not required.)

Army Form C. 2118.

(3)

Place	Date	Hour	Summary of Events and Information	Remarks and references to Appendices
BARLY. CAMP.	June 9th (cont)		Captain T E G NUGENT MC appointed 2nd in command vice MAJOR A F L GORDON MC transferred as 2nd in command to 1st Bn 2nd Lt W D FAULKNER took over duties of A/adjutant. The Commanding Officer inspected camp during the morning.	
	" "	10th	Work on dug outs — Training as per programme. Baths in SOMBRIN were allotted to the Bn throughout the day. A large percentage of the Bn were innoculated.	
		11th	Companies were at the disposal of Coy Comdrs for cleaning up camp etc. At 2 pm the Bn less transport – shoemakers – tailors etc marched to new camp in the grounds of the CHATEAU at BAVINCOURT. The Bn was met by the drums & pipers of the 1st Bn on the outskirts of BAVINCOURT and played into camp. The camp consisted of tents pitched among the trees.	

D. D. & L., London, E.C.
(A8001) Wt. W1 71/M2031 750,000 5/17 Sch. 52 Forms/C2118/14

Instructions regarding War Diaries and Intelligence Summaries are contained in F. S. Regs., Part II. and the Staff Manual respectively. Title pages will be prepared in manuscript.

WAR DIARY
or
INTELLIGENCE SUMMARY.
(Erase heading not required.)

Army Form C. 2118.

2nd Bn Irish Guards

Place	Date	Hour	Summary of Events and Information	Remarks and references to Appendices
BAVINCOURT	June 11th (cont).		The remainder of the day was spent in digging out the inside of the tents for protection against bombs and in camouflaging the tents.	
	12th		Companies were at the disposal of Company Commanders for improvement of camp etc. The 25 NCOs who had been chosen to proceed to the Guards' Depot at CATERHAM were left in BARLY CAMP under the Sergeant Major to be improved in the drill etc.	
	13th		300 O.R. were to be detailed daily as a working party to work under the supervision of the R. ANGLESEA R.E. in the [illegible] lines. [illegible] [illegible] [illegible] [illegible] [illegible]	

A5834 Wt. W4973/M687 750,000 8/16 D. D. & L. Ltd. Forms/C.2118/13.

Army Form C. 2118.

(5)

Instructions regarding War Diaries and Intelligence Summaries are contained in F. S. Regs., Part II. and the Staff Manual respectively. Title pages will be prepared in manuscript.

WAR DIARY
or
~~INTELLIGENCE SUMMARY.~~

(Erase heading not required.)

2nd Bn Irish Guards.

Place	Date	Hour	Summary of Events and Information	Remarks and references to Appendices
BAYENCOURT.	June	14th	Working party as arranged.	
		15th	Working party as arranged During this week a cricket match 2nd Bn v 1st Bn was played 2nd Bn won by about 90 runs. The match was played on the Divisional ground, which is a football ground with a concrete pitch layed down, covered with matting.	
	" "	16th	Work as usual.	
		17th	(Sunday) Work as usual.	
		18th	Work as usual. In the afternoon the return match v 1st Bn was played, but this ended in a draw owing to play having to stop because of the rain.	
	" "	19th	Work as usual, except 150 O.R. paraded instead of the 200 — Those who were excused work paraded for baths.	

A5834 Wt. W4973/M687 750,000 8/16 D. D. & L. Ltd. Forms/C.2118/13.

Army Form C. 2118.

Instructions regarding War Diaries and Intelligence Summaries are contained in F. S. Regs., Part II. and the Staff Manual respectively. Title pages will be prepared in manuscript.

WAR DIARY
or
~~INTELLIGENCE SUMMARY.~~

(Erase heading not required.)

2nd Bn Irish Guards.

(6)

Place	Date	Hour	Summary of Events and Information	Remarks and references to Appendices
BAVINCOURT.	June	20th	150 O.R. paraded for the usual work, the remainder proceeded to the Baths in BAVINCOURT.	
		21st	300 O.R. as detailed worked on the new line	
		22nd	work.	
	" "	23rd	Sunday. Divine Service for R.Cs in BAVINCOURT CHURCH at 10.45 a.m. C of E in Camp at 11.15 a.m.	
			Pte F. Timoney won the open mile in the 2nd Guards Brigade Sports. Pte Kells was 2nd in the open half mile. The Bn Tug of war team (which by misadventure) took part in the 2nd Guards Brigade Sports, won the final easily against 1st Bn Scots Gds.	
	" "	24th	Work as usual.	

A5834 Wt. W4973/M687 750,000 8/16 D. D. & L. Ltd. Forms/C.2118/13.

Instructions regarding War Diaries and Intelligence Summaries are contained in F. S. Regs., Part II. and the Staff Manual respectively. Title pages will be prepared in manuscript.

WAR DIARY
or
~~INTELLIGENCE SUMMARY.~~
(Erase heading not required.)

2nd Bn Irish Guards

Army Form C. 2118.

(7)

Place	Date	Hour	Summary of Events and Information	Remarks and references to Appendices
BAVINCOURT	June	25th	Work as usual In the afternoon the Irish Guards continued to play the Guards Machine Gun Regiment at cricket. The Irish Guards won fairly easly — Scores I.Gds 143 M.G. Regt 125.	
		26th	Work as usual In the afternoon 4th Gds Bde cricket XI played H.Q. Gds Div The match ended in a draw owing to time Scores 4th Gds Bde 199 for 7 wickets (declared) — Div 120 for 8 wickets Capt Nugent & the C.O. played for the 4th Gds Bde 2/Lts G.T. Heaton & J.J.B. BRADY joined the Bn	
		27th	Work as usual 2 pm A lecture on "Co-operation between Tanks & Infantry" was given at BAVINCOURT, to which all officers & NCOs attended. Pte F. Timmins won the open mile in the R.E. Sports Pte O'Shea was 2nd in the open high jump — doing 5 ft 4 ins	

A5834 Wt. W4973/M687 750,000 8/16 D. D. & L. Ltd. Forms/C.2118/13.

Army Form C. 2118.

Instructions regarding War Diaries and Intelligence Summaries are contained in F. S. Regs., Part II. and the Staff Manual respectively. Title pages will be prepared in manuscript.

WAR DIARY
or
~~INTELLIGENCE SUMMARY.~~

(*Erase heading not required.*) 2nd Bn Irish Guards.

(8)

Place	Date	Hour	Summary of Events and Information	Remarks and references to Appendices
BAVINCOURT	June	28th	Work as usual	
			During the day the CO and other commanding Officers of the 4th Guards Brigade motored to WISQUES to look over the ARMY SCHOOL.	
			Pte ARTHUR fought a 10 round contest with another man in the 15th Corps, just losing on points. (Pte Arthur only had 2 days training)	
		29th	Work as usual.	
			The 2nd Bn Scots Gds held their boxing meeting at SOMBRIN to which all ranks of the Gds Div could enter.	
			Pte Hall T won the heavy weights	2nd Bn
			Sgt. Murphy (runner up in the light weights)	
			Pte Howard was runner up in the light heavys	
			Pte Hickie runner up in the feather wts	
			Pte Power also won the 2 miles (open to all) in the Machine Gun Gds sports at SAULTY	
			In the evening, the 1st & 2nd Bns had a dinner to which the Brigadier of the 4th Gd Bde (Gen Butler) came. This dinner of Irish Guardsmen was a great success.	

A5834 Wt. W4973/M687 750,000 8/16 D. D. & L. Ltd. Forms/C.2118/13

Army Form C. 2118.

Instructions regarding War Diaries and Intelligence Summaries are contained in F. S. Regs., Part II. and the Staff Manual respectively. Title pages will be prepared in manuscript.

WAR DIARY
or
~~INTELLIGENCE SUMMARY.~~
(Erase heading not required.) 2nd Bn Irish Guards

(9)

Place	Date	Hour	Summary of Events and Information	Remarks and references to Appendices
BAVINCOURT	June	30th	Sunday Divine Service for R.C. in BAVINCOURT CHURCH at 10.45 am. C of E service was cancelled owing to the sickness of the Clergyman H.R.H. the Duke of CONNAUGHT arrived at 1 pm and lunched with Divisional Headquarters. In the afternoon he inspected some transport and was there had presented to him the Commanding Officers in the Guards Division. In the evening the 1st Bn Irish Guards with Lt Col Alexander & Capt Fox of the 2nd Bn very easily defeated the Gds Div H.Q. A team at cricket. At 8.20 am an advanced party of the Bn consisting of 2nd in C and 50 O.R. proceeded to CRIEL PLAGE by motor lorry where under the direction of the Staff Captain the new camp for the 4th Guards Brigade is under construction.	

A5834 Wt. W4973/M687 750,000 8/16 D. D. & L. Ltd. Forms/C.2118/13

Instructions regarding War Diaries and Intelligence Summaries are contained in F. S. Regs., Part II. and the Staff Manual respectively. Title pages will be prepared in manuscript.

WAR DIARY
or
INTELLIGENCE SUMMARY. 2nd Bn. Irish Guards.
(Erase heading not required.)

Army Form C. 2118.

(10)

Place	Date	Hour	Summary of Events and Information	Remarks and references to Appendices
BAVINCOURT	June 30th	1st – 1918	The whole of this month has been very fine, although not very hot. Every advantage has been taken, owing to the weather and the ground, to encourage all forms of athletics and games. This has met with the very greatest success and has been most beneficial to the Bn. There has been practically no sickness and the men are both healthy and happy. Work has interfered greatly with any training this month, but previous to coming to BAVINCOURT — considerable training was carried out, and valuable instruction given. The training of young NCOs has been carefully seen into. A batch of 20 who have been made this month, are at present under the ~~Sgt~~ S.M. in BARLY CAMP where they are under ~~the~~ instruction in drill and duties. This is going to be most beneficial.	

H. R. Alexander Lt Col
Commanding 2nd Bn
Irish Guards.
2/7/18

A5834 Wt. W4973/M687 750,000 8/16 D. D. & L. Ltd. Forms/C.2118/13

CONFIDENTIAL.

7

WAR DIARY

OF

2nd Bn. Irish Guards.

Vol. VII, 1918.

FROM: 1st July, 1918

TO : 31st July, 1918.

2nd Bn Irish Guards

Instructions regarding War Diaries and Intelligence Summaries are contained in F. S. Regs., Part II. and the Staff Manual respectively. Title pages will be prepared in manuscript.

WAR DIARY
or
~~INTELLIGENCE SUMMARY~~.

(Erase heading not required.)

Army Form C. 2118.

Place	Date	Hour	Summary of Events and Information	Remarks and references to Appendices
BAVINCOURT	July 1st	8am	The Battalion found the usual working parties. Work commenced at 8 am and finished at about 12 noon. The Commanding Officer walked over to the Details Camp early and watched the squad of young Corporals drilling under the Sergeant Major. He afterwards went on to the digging, himself taking a spade.	
"	July 2nd	8am	Usual working parties in the morning. Our men always seemed to finish their task before anyone else, & so were always able to get back to Camp in time for dinners.	
		2.30pm	In the afternoon several Officers went over to the 1st Guards Brigade Racemeeting which was held in a field N of the LA CAUCHIE-GAUDIEMPRE ROAD. The Bn had only one starter "THE MULE" in the 1½ miles hurdle race for ponies. Capt A.R.S NUTTING MC rode a good race but though he managed to get away well, there were 3 other ponies	

A5834 Wt. W4973/M687 750,000 8/16 D. D. & L. Ltd. Forms/C.2118/13

WAR DIARY

or

~~INTELLIGENCE~~ SUMMARY.

(Erase heading not required.)

Army Form C. 2118.

Instructions regarding War Diaries and Intelligence Summaries are contained in F. S. Regs., Part II. and the Staff Manual respectively. Title pages will be prepared in manuscript.

Place	Date	Hour	Summary of Events and Information	Remarks and references to Appendices
BAVINCOURT	JULY 2nd		that were too good and he finished fourth. One of the chief features of the meeting was the Major General winning a race on his own horse. There were several bookies including Lt M.R. HELY-HUTCHINSON MC (late adjt 2nd Bn) & CAPT R.E. SASSOON MC. The latter as usual did quite good trade, and appeared to be giving better odds. A very enjoyable day.	
BAVINCOURT	JULY 3rd	1a	There were no working parties to-day and the Bn went to the Baths which were much needed. Nothing of any interest happened. All this time the advanced party which had gone on to CRIEL PLAGE were slaving away in order to have the camp ready for the advent of the Bn.	
"	July 4th		'American Independence' day. Great excitement among the Americans. Good fellowship everywhere. The 2nd in Command	

A5834 Wt. W4973/M687 750,000 8/16 D. D. & L. Ltd. Forms/C.2118/13

Instructions regarding War Diaries and Intelligence Summaries are contained in F. S. Regs., Part II. and the Staff Manual respectively. Title pages will be prepared in manuscript.

WAR DIARY
or
INTELLIGENCE SUMMARY.
(Erase heading not required.)

Army Form C. 2118.

Place	Date	Hour	Summary of Events and Information	Remarks and references to Appendices
			had a narrow escape as he was nearly hit by a baseball which luckily just missed him and struck a V.A.D in the face.	
			The Battalion found the usual working parties	
Kuby Bavincourt.	July 5th.		Usual working parties. We were now enjoying extremely pleasant weather. Bright sunshine with a refreshing breeze, which tempered the heat. Work for the day was always over by dinner and the men had the rest of the day to themselves.	
"	July 6th.		Usual working parties. In the afternoon the 1st Bn Kindly invited us to watch an athletic Contest between themselves & the 1st Bn Munster Regt. The contests included tug o war 100 yds Qr mile ½ mile 1 mile.	

A5834 Wt. W4973/M687 750,000 8/16 D. D. & L. Ltd. Forms/C.2118/13

Army Form C. 2118.

Instructions regarding War Diaries and Intelligence Summaries are contained in F. S. Regs., Part II. and the Staff Manual respectively. Title pages will be prepared in manuscript.

WAR DIARY
or
INTELLIGENCE SUMMARY.
(Erase heading not required.)

Place	Date	Hour	Summary of Events and Information	Remarks and references to Appendices
			Except for the 100 yds which was won by Lcpl STOREY (whose other name is GEORGE) of the MUNSTERS, the 1st Bn were successful in every contest. A very good performance. The tug o war was particularly exciting. The 1st Bn just managed to pull their opponents over ~~~~ in the final pull.	
Bavincourt	July 7th		The day being Sunday Father F.M. BROWNE conducted MASS in BAVINCOURT CHURCH at 10 a.m. The Church of England party had divine service in the officers lines at 11.30 am. Nothing of special interest occurred.	
"	July 8th		Coys were at the disposal of Coy commanders in the morning for practice in march discipline. The rest of the day was taken up with preparations for the move. Orders had been received for a party to proceed to PARIS to help to form a Composite Bn for the celebrations	

A5834 Wt. W4973/M687 750,000 8/16 D. D. & L. Ltd. Forms/C.2118/13

Instructions regarding War Diaries and Intelligence Summaries are contained in F. S. Regs., Part II. and the Staff Manual respectively. Title pages will be prepared in manuscript.

WAR DIARY
or
INTELLIGENCE SUMMARY.
(Erase heading not required.)

Army Form C. 2118.

Place	Date	Hour	Summary of Events and Information	Remarks and references to Appendices
			on July 14th. (SEE NARRATIVE ATTACHED).	
BAVINCOURT	July 5th.		The 'PARIS PARTY' started early catching the 9 am from MONDICOURT STATION. The Battalion moved to CRIEL PLAGE by rail starting at 2pm. Bn HQRs were somewhat depleted ~~during~~ for the move as the Commanding Officer, adjutant, ass't adjutant, Sergeant major, medical officer, sick sergeant, Orderly Room clerk, signalling sergeant, mess sergeant and all the drummers had gone to PARIS; and the 2nd in Command had gone on with the advanced party. CAPT A.R.S NUTTING MC, therefore Commanded the Bn. The journey was uneventful. Dinners were had before starting and teas at MONDICOURT station. EU was reached at about 2.30 am. The men had some hot tea before marching off to camp a distance of about 9 KM.	

A5834 Wt. W4973/M687 750,000 8/16 D. D. & L. Ltd. Forms/C.2118/13

Army Form C. 2118.

Instructions regarding War Diaries and Intelligence Summaries are contained in F. S. Regs., Part II. and the Staff Manual respectively. Title pages will be prepared in manuscript.

WAR DIARY
or
INTELLIGENCE SUMMARY.

(Erase heading not required.)

Place	Date	Hour	Summary of Events and Information	Remarks and references to Appendices
~~July 10th~~ CRIEL PLAGE	JULY 10th		Camp was reached at about 6am, & the men had breakfasts. The rest of the day was spent in cleaning up, feet inspections, making tents comfortable etc. The C.O attended a Conference at Bde HQrs, ~~at[illegible]~~ to discuss the training of the "Young Officers" when they arrived.	
"	July 11th		Practically the whole of the Battalion were detailed as working parties under the RE, working on the CAMP. They were employed on erecting marquees, making washhouses, digging wells etc. The hours of work were from 9 am to 12 noon and from 1.30 pm to 4.30 pm	
"	July 12th		The Brigade issued orders that bathing was only allowed at low tide. The men were very pleased with the new place and enjoyed the B bathing. The same working parties were again detailed. The remainder of the Bn were employed on erecting the tents and generally cleaning up the camp.	

A5834 Wt. W4973/M687 750,000 8/16 D. D. & L. Ltd. Forms/C.2118/13

Instructions regarding War Diaries and Intelligence Summaries are contained in F. S. Regs., Part II. and the Staff Manual respectively. Title pages will be prepared in manuscript.

WAR DIARY

or

INTELLIGENCE SUMMARY.

(Erase heading not required.)

Army Form C. 2118.

Place	Date	Hour	Summary of Events and Information	Remarks and references to Appendices
~~[illegible]~~ CRILL PLACE "	JULY 13th		Coys did one hours drill under their Coy Commanders during the morning. They had had no facilities for drill for a considerable time, and were consequently very much out of practice. Working parties were required to work under the RE as usual.	
	July 14th		Sunday. There was a Bde Church parade for Church of England Service. Owing to the inclement weather the service was held in a large marquee. The Rev CK BEST MC Chaplain to the 4th Bn Grenadier Guards officiated. The Army Commander, General Sir Henry Rawlinson GCB etc was present at the service. He afterwards inspected camp and expressed himself as pleased with the appearance of the men and the state of the camp. He showed special interest in the cooking arrangements & diet sheet, asking many questions,	

A5834 Wt. W4973/M687 750,000 8/16 D. D. & L. Ltd. Forms/C.2118/13

Army Form C. 2118.

Instructions regarding War Diaries and Intelligence Summaries are contained in F. S. Regs., Part II. and the Staff Manual respectively. Title pages will be prepared in manuscript.

WAR DIARY
or
INTELLIGENCE SUMMARY.
(Erase heading not required.)

Place	Date	Hour	Summary of Events and Information	Remarks and references to Appendices
CRIEL PLAGE	July 15th		Coys were at the disposal of Coy Commanders for close order and arm drill. The one thing we lack at this Camp is a good parade ground near at hand. As the Camp is on the slope of a hill there are no level space on which to drill. The grass is very thick also usual fatigue parties detailed. On the advice of the Army Commander all tents were dug down to a depth of about 18" inches. This gives more room and also provides shelter against the wind	
	July 16th		From 9am to 10am Coys did close order & arm drill under their Coy Commdrs. From 10.30am to 12 noon Coys did open order drill, practice in march discipline etc. Signallers also paraded for instruction under their signalling Corporal. Usual camp routine	

A5834 Wt. W4973/M687 750,000 8/16 D. D. & L. Ltd. Forms/C.2118/13

Army Form C. 2118.

Instructions regarding War Diaries and Intelligence Summaries are contained in F. S. Regs., Part II. and the Staff Manual respectively. Title pages will be prepared in manuscript.

WAR DIARY
or
~~INTELLIGENCE SUMMARY.~~

(Erase heading not required.)

Place	Date	Hour	Summary of Events and Information	Remarks and references to Appendices
CRIEL PLAGE	July 17th		Large working parties were detailed. No training was therefore possible. A great deal of work however was done in levelling the ground in front of the cook houses and filling in some old trenches which had evidently been started by BELGIANS. They were not very good trenches so ~~[illegible]~~ one felt any qualms about filling them in.	
	July 18th		The Paris party suddenly arrived very early in the morning although we had been informed that they would not arrive for another two days. They had had a long railway journey and were consequently tired. Nothing very much was done during the day.	
	July 19th		Large working parties were ordered, so there were no men for training. In the evening the 4th Bn Grenadier Guards gave a dinner party, it being the anniversary of their formation. The ~~[illegible]~~ Commanding	

A5834 Wt. W4973/M687 750,000 8/16 D. D. & L. Ltd. Forms/C.2118/13

Army Form C. 2118.

Instructions regarding War Diaries and Intelligence Summaries are contained in F. S. Regs., Part II. and the Staff Manual respectively. Title pages will be prepared in manuscript.

WAR DIARY
or
~~INTELLIGENCE~~ SUMMARY.
(Erase heading not required.)

Place	Date	Hour	Summary of Events and Information	Remarks and references to Appendices
			Officer and the 2nd in Command attended and appeared to Enjoy themselves	
CRIEL PLAGE	July 20th		The Brigadier inspected Camp in the morning. As it came on to rain just as he was starting so he waited in the second sick tent. There were some very well executed designs outside the lines made of stones chalk, broken glass etc. The Camp was very clean and in good order. In the afternoon the CO 2nd in C + Capt Nutting went into DIEPPE to buy stock for the dry canteen.	
	July 21st		Sunday. Divine service as usual for all denominations. The Commanding Officer had toothache so went to see the dentist at the American hospital. While he was	

A5834 Wt. W4973/M687 750,000 8/16 D. D. & L. Ltd. Forms/C.2118/13

Instructions regarding War Diaries and Intelligence Summaries are contained in F. S. Regs., Part II. and the Staff Manual respectively. Title pages will be prepared in manuscript.

WAR DIARY
or
INTELLIGENCE SUMMARY.
(Erase heading not required.)

Army Form C. 2118.

Place	Date	Hour	Summary of Events and Information	Remarks and references to Appendices
CRIEL PLAGE			there an officer came in and had a tooth out. The dentist did not appear to give him any sort of anaesthetic either local or otherwise the officer seemed not to mind.	
	July 22nd		Coys were at the disposal of their Coy Commanders for drill inspections etc during the morning. Ordinary working parties for the improvement of Camp	
	July 23rd		A very wet day. The Commanding Officer had intended to have a "B" parade in clean fatigue dress to pick out some athletes but owing to the very inclement weather this was abandoned. The same party as on ~~Tuesday~~ Saturday journeyed again to DIEPPE to buy stock for the Regt Canteen	

A5834 Wt. W4973/M687 750,000 8/16 D. D. & L. Ltd. Forms/C.2118/13

WAR DIARY
or
INTELLIGENCE SUMMARY.
(*Erase heading not required.*)

Army Form C. 2118.

Instructions regarding War Diaries and Intelligence Summaries are contained in F. S. Regs., Part II. and the Staff Manual respectively. Title pages will be prepared in manuscript.

Place	Date	Hour	Summary of Events and Information	Remarks and references to Appendices
CRIEL PLACE	July 24th		The Battalion paraded in clean fatigue dress at 9am and the Commanding officer made each man run a hundred yards and throw a cricket ball. He ran the 100 yards in platoon heats & picked out the best runner in each heat. In this way several unknown runners were discovered. At 6 o'clock in the evening all runners who had been picked out in the morning assembled on the cricket ground and were run against each other, the Commanding Officer finally selecting about 20 runners & jumpers who were put into training for the Brigade sports.	
	July 25th		Lieut CR Hamilton joined the Battalion from England and was posted to No 1 Company. Coys were at the disposal of Coy Commanders for drill etc. Usual fatigue parties ordered.	

A5834 Wt. W4973/M687 750,000 8/16 D. D. & L. Ltd. Forms/C.2118/13

Instructions regarding War Diaries and Intelligence Summaries are contained in F. S. Regs., Part II. and the Staff Manual respectively. Title pages will be prepared in manuscript.

WAR DIARY
or
INTELLIGENCE SUMMARY.
(Erase heading not required.)

Army Form C. 2118.

Place	Date	Hour	Summary of Events and Information	Remarks and references to Appendices
CRIEL PLAGE	July 26th		The Commanding Officer took 5 Officers out and prepared a scheme for the Defence of a Locality. This scheme was in preparation of the arrival of the Young Officers who were going to be attached to us. A showery day, with a great deal of wind.	
	July 27th		All men who had not been innoculated within the last 12 months were innoculated during the day. We heard that about 150 of the "Young Officers" were arriving that evening. However they did not turn up but for some reason were taken on to ROUEN.	
	July 28th		Sunday. Usual service. 150 "Young Officers" Officers arrived of whom ~~about~~ 27 were posted to the Bn. They were all newly Commissioned though some had had considerable service in the ranks. Lieut CR Hamilton was put in charge of the company with Lieuts Black 2Lts Dasser Brookes and Kent as platoon commanders.	
	July 29th		The Brigadier gave an opening address to the Young Officers in the Casino. In the afternoon the Commanding Officer motored into DIEPPE to buy some running stores.	

A5834 Wt. W4973/M687 750,000 8/16 D. D. & L. Ltd. Forms/C.2118/13

Instructions regarding War Diaries and Intelligence Summaries are contained in F. S. Regs., Part II. and the Staff Manual respectively. Title pages will be prepared in manuscript.

WAR DIARY
or
~~INTELLIGENCE SUMMARY.~~
(Erase heading not required.)

Army Form C. 2118.

Place	Date	Hour	Summary of Events and Information	Remarks and references to Appendices
RIEL PLACE	July 30th		Usual working parties in the morning. In the evening ~~the~~ the C.O held a trial to find the best sprinters in the Bn for the sports. 100 yds was run. Sgt Murphy won with Pte McGuire and Sgt Wain 2nd & 3rd respectively	
	31st		The Commanding Officer made final choice as to who was to represent the Bn at the sports. The final team was selected as follows. MILE: C.O, Capt Law, Sgt Gilmartin ½ mile: Pte Timmony, C.O, Pte McAree ¼ mile: Pte Hills, Sgt Wain, Pte Pollock Relay race: Sgt Murphy, Pte McGuire, Pte Hill, Pte Timmony 100 yds: Sgt Murphy, Pte McGuire, Sgt Wain	

E.H. Nugent Major/Lt Col
Cmdg 2/Irish Guards

A5834 Wt. W4973/M687 750,000 8/16 D. D. & L. Ltd. Forms/C.2118/13

REPORT

on the
CEREMONIAL PARADE IN PARIS, BRITISH COMPOSITE BATTALION.
* = * = * = * = * = * = * = * =

JULY 10th - JULY 16th, 1918.

COMPOSITION. 1.
The Composite Battalion was to be formed at ROMESCAMP. The first detachments arrived on the early morning of July 10th, and the last on the early morning of July 12th. So the complete Battn. was formed by the 12th July.
(See Appendix "A".)

PARADES. were heldevery day and included :-
1. Sizeing companies and platoons.
2. Inspection and cleaning of dress and equipment.
3. Arm Drill - especially "fixing bayonets"-"presenting arms" "sloping arms"- "ordering arms"- "unfixing bayonets".
4. Marching past in "fours", Column of platoons, and "column of half platoons".
5. Teaching Officers to give the words of command on the correct foot.

All detachments showed great keenness, and their improvement in drill after a few parades was most marked.

CAMP. consisted of ordinary bell-tents and marquees. Everything possible was done by the Camp authorities for the comfort of Officers and men.

ENTRAINMENT. 2.
The Battalion paraded in Camp at 6 P.M., July 12th, and marched to ABANCOURT STATION.
Entrained at 7 P.M.
Train departed at 8.10 P.M.
There was ample room for the Battalion on the train, which was composed of 1st, 2nd, and 3rd Class compartments, horse vans, baggage vans, etc.
(Appendix "B".)

DETRAINMENT. 3.
Arrived at the CHAMP de MARS ST. PARIS on July 13th at 6 A.M.
There the Battalion was met by an Officer of the 134 Regiment of French Infantry, a guide and Lieut. ~~Fourbie~~ FURBY, Guards Division Interpreter.
The French Authorities made all arrangements for transportation of Baggage.

ARRIVAL. 4.
The Battalion marched to the GRAND PALAIS. Everything possible had been done by the French Authorities for the comfort of the Battn.
(a) RATIONS. French cooks and cookers with ample rations were detailed and ready to feed the men - hot coffee was supplied at once on arrival.
1 litre of red wine per man per day was issued and on July 14th a bottle of champagne amongst 4 was issued in addition.
(b) BILLETING. Every man had a wired bed, palliasse and blankets.
(c) WASHING ETC. Latrines, washing places, etc, had been erected ready for use.
(d) FATIGUES. French soldiers had been detailed to keep the quarters clean, and dispose of all rubbish.
(e) OFFICERS QUARTERS. Billets were set aside for Officers on duty in the Grand Palais. Private flats in the AV. MONTAIGNE had been requisitioned for Officers.

ARRIVAL.(Ctd) 4.
(f).TELEPHONE. The Commandant of the Grand Palais handed over his private bureau and telephone for the use of the Commanding Officer.

Standing Orders were issued to the Battalion.
(Appendix "C".)

Whilst in Paris, Companies held one parade in the morning under Company arrangements, otherwise the men, except those on Duty, were free.

CONFERENCE. 5.
At 4 P.M. July 13th all Officers Commanding Detachments of the Allies attended a Conference at the INVALIDES presided over by GENERAL VALDANT. Orders were issued and the parade was explained.
(Appendix "D")

Commanding Officers were then presented to General Guillaumat, Military Governor of Paris.

It is interesting to note, that a definite formation in the march past was laid down, namely double colums of fours. This was insisted on for two reasons. (1) In order that the Column should not be too long. (2) To ensure of sufficient thickness in the column to prevent the column from getting broken by the crowds during the march past. This formation to my knowledge has never been adopted by us before, but it was undoubtedly a very great success, and is extremely spectacular.

The Commanding Officer called a meeting of Company Officers, Sergeant Major and Drill Sgts., and the orders, march past, etc., were explained, and final details arranged for the Review.

THE CEREMONIAL PARADE.

PARADE. 1.
The Battalion paraded in Marching Order at 6.45 A.M. July 14th Marched from Barracks at 7.15 A.M. and was ready in position at 8.30 A.M.

ASSEMBLY. 2.
At 8.30 A.M. General Guillaumat rode down the lines and was received by the General Salute. Band and Drums as per order did not play.

INSPECTION.3. At 9 A.M. The President drove past in his carriage - troops presented arms.

PRESENTATION =OF= DECORATIONS. 4. Immediately the President had passed, Officers and O.R., as detailed, fell out and were decorated by the President, opposite the Saluting base, falling in again, after the saluting base had been passed.

MARCH PAST. 5.
All Units now got into position, ready to march past.
At 9.30 A.M. the march commenced.
The Battalion marched past as shown on diagram.
As per order, bands did not play until within 100 yards of the saluting point.
On reaching a point about 500 yards past the saluting point, detachments of the Allies were then allowed to continue playing.

ROUTE.
AVENUE de BOULOGNE - To the left up the AV.MALAKOF - B.HAUSMANN - PLACE de la CONCORDE into the Garden of the TUILLERIES, where spaces were set aside for Units to have 20 minutes rest. Units then marched back to Barracks independently.

Throughout the whole march past which lasted for 1½ Hrs, the Battn. marched with fixed bayonets, at "attention", changing arms at various periods.

REMARKS. 6.
The Battalion marched past extremely well and was very well received by the people, flowers were thrown and given to the men, and the crowds cheered the whole length of the march.

REMARKS.(Contd) 6.

The Band and Drums and Pipes took it in turn to play continuously.

It is perhaps very gratifying to know, according to the French papers and from French Officers that the British detachment was considered by far the best on parade. Another point of interest was the reason of the lateness of orders, or knowledge of where the parade was to take place, and the route chosen - which I was given to understand was owing to the German Gun firing on Paris at the time.

DEPARTURE.

IN PARIS. The Battalion remained in Paris until the morning of the 16th July.

DEPARTURE. 1.

The Battalion paraded in Barracks at 7.45 A.M.
Marched off at 8 A.M.
Entrained at 9 A.M.
Train left at 11.30 A.M.
There was ample accommodation in 1st, 2nd, and 3rd Class Compartments. (Appendix "E".)

BREAK UP OF BATTALION. 2. The Battalion was broken up by detachments detraining at their various destinations.

REMARKS. 3.

I should like to add that everything possible was done for the Battalion by the British Authorities as regards the comfort of the Battalion during our stay at ROMESCAMP, and during the journey to and from Paris, also whilst in Paris.

And also for the great kindness and trouble taken by the French Authorities during the stay of the Battalion in Paris.

All detachments of the British Composite Battalion showed great keenness, behaved very well thourghout the whole period and did everything in their power to make the parade the success it was.

W. Faulkner Capt. & Adjt.
for Lieut. Col.
2nd Battn. Irish Guards.
Commanding British Composite Battalion.

July 23rd, 1918.

S E C R E T.

W A R D I A R Y.

2 N D. B N. I R I S H G U A R D S.

VOLUME VIII.

(1918.)

Period :-

AUGUST 1ST. to 31ST. 1918.

9 l 38

Army Form C. 2118.

WAR DIARY
or
~~INTELLIGENCE SUMMARY.~~

(Erase heading not required.)

Instructions regarding War Diaries and Intelligence Summaries are contained in F. S. Regs., Part II. and the Staff Manual respectively. Title pages will be prepared in manuscript.

Place	Date	Hour	Summary of Events and Information	Remarks and references to Appendices
CRIEL PLAGE	August 1st		Coys were at the disposal of Coy Commanders during the morning for drill, Lewis Gun instruction &c. Fatigue parties were ordered for improvement of Camp etc.	
	August 2nd		Coys were at the disposal of Coy Commanders for usual routine. Usual working parties ordered. Training for the Sports on the following day was in full swing. The B^n fancied its chance of doing well.	
	August 3rd		4th Guards Brigade Athletic Sports took place. The Battalion covered itself with glory. See programme attached. They won every single event that counted points & got every place except 2nd & 3rd in the hundred yards, 3rd in the ¼ mile, 2nd in the mile & 3rd in the throwing the Cricket	

A5834 Wt. W4973/M687 750,000 8/16 D. D. & L. Ltd. Forms/C.2118/13

WAR DIARY
or
~~INTELLIGENCE SUMMARY.~~
(Erase heading not required.)

Army Form C. 2118.

(2)

Instructions regarding War Diaries and Intelligence Summaries are contained in F. S. Regs., Part II. and the Staff Manual respectively. Title pages will be prepared in manuscript.

Place	Date	Hour	Summary of Events and Information	Remarks and references to Appendices
CRIEL PLAGE	Aug 13th		fall. The Bn won the Bde championship with 37 points ~~[illegible]~~ With 3rd Bn Coldstream Guards & 4th Bn Grenadier Guards Equal 2nd with 3 points each and the Trench Mortar Battery 3rd with 2 points	
	Aug 14th		Sunday. There was a Bde parade service in Commemoration of the outbreak of war. An impressive service was held. Rev Hawkes preached the sermon, which was well received.	
	Aug 15th		Coys were at the disposal of Company Commanders during the morning. Usual working parties were ordered. Designs for a Guards Divisional Christmas Card were asked for with no result.	
	Aug 16th		The Commanding Officer gave a demonstration to the Bn of the new platoon organisation in the morning. Usual fatigue parties were ordered.	

A5834 Wt. W4973/M687 750,000 8/16 D. D. & L. Ltd. Forms/C.2118/13

(8)

Army Form C. 2118.

WAR DIARY
or
~~INTELLIGENCE SUMMARY.~~
(Erase heading not required.)

Instructions regarding War Diaries and Intelligence Summaries are contained in F. S. Regs., Part II. and the Staff Manual respectively. Title pages will be prepared in manuscript.

Place	Date	Hour	Summary of Events and Information	Remarks and references to Appendices
CRILL PLAGE	Aug 7th		Coy Commanders took their NCOs out in the morning for a tactical scheme on Mt JOLI BOIS. Usual fatigue parties. In the evening Col Campbell of the GHQ BAYONET FIGHTING SCHOOL gave a lecture to the Bde. He advocated "blood + iron" to a certain extent. The men who had been innoculated on July 26th & 27th were done again.	
	Aug 8th		Coys were at the disposal of Company Commanders in the morning for drill, Lewis Gun instruction etc. Usual fatigue parties were ordered.	
	Aug 9th		Usual Routine and fatigue parties. Bathing was in full swing at this time. Each morning before breakfast the Commanding Officer, 2nd in Command, adjutant, asst adjt, Transport Officer and Quartermaster might be seen skipping lightly down the sea to their morning dip, which some of them said they enjoyed.	
	Aug 10th		Usual routine and fatigue parties.	

Instructions regarding War Diaries and Intelligence Summaries are contained in F. S. Regs., Part II. and the Staff Manual respectively. Title pages will be prepared in manuscript.

WAR DIARY
or
~~INTELLIGENCE~~ SUMMARY.
(Erase heading not required.)

Army Form C. 2118.

(4)

Place	Date	Hour	Summary of Events and Information	Remarks and references to Appendices
CLIFF PARK	Aug 11th		Sunday. All denominations had Divine Service. After Church the Commanding Officer inspected Camp. A peaceful day.	
	Aug 12th		Coys were at the disposal of Company Commanders during the morning for drill, Lewis Gun instruction etc. The Commanding Officer suggested to ~~the~~ the Battalion Athletic Team, that they should have Bn NOVICES Athletic Sports. The Sports were to be run entirely by the Athletic Team. The suggestion was accepted & preparations were started at once. Each Coy was to be allowed to enter a team of 3 in each event.	
	Aug 13th		Nos 1 & 2 Coys paraded for Bayonet Fighting under QMSI ELLIOTT, A.G.S. late of WARLEY BKS. Nos 3 & 4 Coys were at the disposal of the Company Commanders.	

A5834 Wt. W4973/M687 750,000 8/16 D. D. & L. Ltd. Forms/C.2118/13

Army Form C. 2118.

Instructions regarding War Diaries and Intelligence Summaries are contained in F. S. Regs., Part II. and the Staff Manual respectively. Title pages will be prepared in manuscript.

WAR DIARY
or
~~INTELLIGENCE SUMMARY.~~
(Erase heading not required.)

Place	Date	Hour	Summary of Events and Information	Remarks and references to Appendices
CRIEL PLAGE	Aug 14th		The Battalion paraded at 9 am for a Route March. ROUTE. CRIEL - LE QUESNAY - MESNIL VAL - CRIEL PLAGE. Lt Col T L Reid OBE late Commanding Officer of the Bn ~~[illegible]~~ visited the Bn in the morning and remained to luncheon. In the afternoon the pipers came and played in Battalion HQRS. Strict orders were given out about bathing as there had been accidents.	
	Aug 15th		No 3 & 4 Coys paraded under QMSI ELLIOTT for Bayonet fighting. No 1 & 2 Coys were at the disposal of their Coy Commanders for drill etc. Usual fatigue parties were ordered. The Bn played association football against the attached [illegible] in the evening winning 5 goals to 1.	

A5834 Wt. W4973/M687 750,000 8/16 D. D. & L. Ltd. Forms/C.2118/13

WAR DIARY
or
~~INTELLIGENCE~~ SUMMARY.

(Erase heading not required.)

Instructions regarding War Diaries and Intelligence Summaries are contained in F. S. Regs., Part II. and the Staff Manual respectively. Title pages will be prepared in manuscript.

Army Form C. 2118.

(6)

Place	Date	Hour	Summary of Events and Information	Remarks and references to Appendices
CRIEL PLAGE	Aug 11th		The whole Bn paraded in clean fatigue dress at 9 am for identification purposes as a man said to belong to the Bn had misbehaved himself in MESNIL VAL. However no man was identified. The Commanding Officer inspected the clothing, kits etc of each Coy in turn and found same in good repair.	
	Aug 17th		The Adjutant held a parade in the morning. All tents were pitched as the authorities feared a raid by Hostile Aircraft.	
	Aug 18th		Sunday. Usual Divine Service. The Commanding Officer inspected camp after Church.	
	Aug 19th		A short musketry course was started. Each Coy had the range for 2 hours where they did one grouping and two application practices.	

A5834 Wt. W4973/M687 750,000 8/16 D. D. & L. Ltd. Forms/C.2118/13

Army Form C. 2118.

(7)

WAR DIARY
or
~~INTELLIGENCE~~ SUMMARY.
(Erase heading not required.)

Instructions regarding War Diaries and Intelligence Summaries are contained in F. S. Regs., Part II. and the Staff Manual respectively. Title pages will be prepared in manuscript.

Place	Date	Hour	Summary of Events and Information	Remarks and references to Appendices
CRIEL PLAGE	Aug 26th		The musketry course was continued in the morning. In the afternoon the Bn held an athletic meeting for N.C.O.s & men which was a great success. They were run in a similar way to the Brigade Sports that is a Coy [illegible] each Coy was allowed to enter 3 men for each event. No 1 Coy won the inter coy challenge shield, H.Qrs were second and No 2 Coy were third. A copy of the programme is attached.	
	Aug 27th		The Commanding Officer proceeded on leave in the morning the 2nd in Command taking over command of the Battalion. There was an adjutant's parade at 9.30 am after which two companies proceeded to [illegible] for Coy training while the two remaining Coys [illegible] did P & B T under Q.M.S. Elliott.	
	Aug 28th		Two Coys did 1 hours of P & B T & 3 hours Coy training during the morning. The other two Coys did a short Route march.	

A5834 Wt. W4973/M687 750,000 8/16 D. D. & L. Ltd. Forms/C.2118/13

Instructions regarding War Diaries and Intelligence Summaries are contained in F. S. Regs., Part II. and the Staff Manual respectively. Title pages will be prepared in manuscript.

WAR DIARY
or
~~INTELLIGENCE~~ SUMMARY.

(Erase heading not required.)

Army Form C. 2118.

(8)

Place	Date	Hour	Summary of Events and Information	Remarks and references to Appendices
	Aug 22nd		Colonel Campbell DSO GHQ P&BT School lectured to all officers of the Brigade on Recreational TRAINING. He advocated games very strongly. He pointed out how well the great boxers etc had done in the war. He quoted the case of his own sergeant major Jimmy O'DRISCOLL who, he said, had been offered some large ~~fight~~ purses to box. He however refused them and joined the Welsh Horse after about 2½ years of war because he could not be out of it!! When he found after another year or so that the Welsh Horse weren't going out to France he very gallantly transferred to the GHQ P&BT School. We all held our breath at the description of such a brave man!!	
	Aug 23rd		An adjutant's parade in the morning. Also a court martial. Otherwise nothing of interest happened.	

A5834 Wt. W4973/M687 750,000 8/16 D. D. & L. Ltd. Forms/C.2118/13

Army Form C. 2118.

(9)

Instructions regarding War Diaries and Intelligence Summaries are contained in F. S. Regs., Part II. and the Staff Manual respectively. Title pages will be prepared in manuscript.

WAR DIARY
or
~~INTELLIGENCE SUMMARY.~~

(Erase heading not required.)

Place	Date	Hour	Summary of Events and Information	Remarks and references to Appendices
ORIEL PLAGE	Aug 24th		No 1 & 2 Coys paraded at 9 am for P&BT. No 3 & 4 paraded at 10.30 am for the same exercise.	
			Nos 1 & 2 Coys afterwards went for a short route march.	
			A working party was asked to do something in regard to a Church Army hut	
	Aug 25th		Sunday. Usual Divine Services. The Commanding Officer inspected Camp after church.	
	Aug 26th		Each Coy had 1 hours P&BT in the morning. In the afternoon the musketry course was continued.	
			All Coys bathed in the morning.	
			In the evening the preliminary bouts of the Brigade Novices Boxing Competition took place. The Bn did well getting 10 men into the semifinals. All boxed well showing plenty of dash. In most cases they knocked their men out in the first or second round.	

A5834 Wt. W4973/M687 750,000 8/16 D. D. & L. Ltd. Forms/C.2118/13

Army Form C. 2118.

(10)

Instructions regarding War Diaries and Intelligence Summaries are contained in F. S. Regs., Part II. and the Staff Manual respectively. Title pages will be prepared in manuscript.

WAR DIARY
or
~~INTELLIGENCE~~ SUMMARY.

(Erase heading not required.)

Place	Date	Hour	Summary of Events and Information	Remarks and references to Appendices
CRILLE PLACE	Aug 27		Musketry Course continued in the morning. In the afternoon the semi-finals and finals of the Boxing Competition took place. The Bn again did well. They had the winners & runners up in the light weight, welter weight and middle weight, and the winner up in the light heavy weight. A good performance. Programme attached. It being the last evening of the attached officers – a Concert was given by the attached officers. A very merry evening, which was kept up till 4 a.m.	
	Aug 28th		Coys went out and did Coy training with their Coy Commanders in the morning.	
	Aug 2[illegible]		The Commanding Officer took all officers out and did a scheme [illegible] the morning. In the evening a bombshell fell in the shape of an	

A5834 Wt. W4973/M687 750,000 8/16 D. D. & L. Ltd. Forms/C.2118/13

Army Form C. 2118.

(11)

Instructions regarding War Diaries and Intelligence Summaries are contained in F. S. Regs., Part II. and the Staff Manual respectively. Title pages will be prepared in manuscript.

WAR DIARY
or
INTELLIGENCE SUMMARY.

(Erase heading not required.)

Place	Date	Hour	Summary of Events and Information	Remarks and references to Appendices
PLACE			Nov [illegible] 4 [illegible] 1150 OR to proceed [illegible] a draft to the 1st Bn	
	Aug [illegible]		The morning was spent in fitting out the draft [illegible] was to proceed on the following day. In the afternoon the draft was paid.	
	Aug [illegible]		The draft proceeded at [illegible] am. It was one of the [illegible] [illegible] imaginable. In all 1007 OR went from the [illegible]. A [illegible] incident happened when the draft was marching through MESNIL VAL on their way to the station. A man who had lost his cap the day previously had had to parade in steel helmet [illegible] the [illegible] was passing through MESNIL VAL an old lady emerged from a house with the man's cap complete and solemnly presented it to him to the delight of the rest of the Battalion	
			[illegible] [illegible] Commandant [illegible] [illegible] Guards	

A5834 Wt. W4973/M687 750,000 8/16 D. D. & L. Ltd. Forms/C.2118/13

CONFIDENTIAL.

W A R D I A R Y

of

2nd Bn. I R I S H G U A R D S

Vol. IX, 1918.

PERIOD:

From 1st Sept.

To 30th Sept. 1918.

(1)

Army Form C. 2118.

Instructions regarding War Diaries and Intelligence Summaries are contained in F. S. Regs., Part II. and the Staff Manual respectively. Title pages will be prepared in manuscript.

WAR DIARY
or
~~INTELLIGENCE SUMMARY~~. 2nd Bn Irish Guards

(*Erase heading not required.*)

Place	Date	Hour	Summary of Events and Information	Remarks and references to Appendices
CRIEL PLAGE	Sept 1st		Sunday. Usual church services. The Commanding Officer inspected camp after divine service.	
	Sept 2nd		Battalion parade in the morning. In the afternoon the range was allotted to the Battalion. HQRs were having a competition.	
	Sept 3rd		Range again allotted in the morning. Coys also did 1 hours steady drill under Coy arrangements.	
	Sept 4th		The Battalion paraded for Physical and Bayonet training at 9 am and then again for Lewis Gun instruction at 10.30 am. The Commanding Officer took all officers out for a scheme.	
	Sept 5th		N.C.O's did a tactical scheme under their Coy Commanders. The armourer sergeant inspected all the rifles of the Battalion.	

A5834 Wt. W4973/M687 750,000 8/16 D. D. & L. Ltd. Forms/C.2118/13

Instructions regarding War Diaries and Intelligence Summaries are contained in F. S. Regs., Part II. and the Staff Manual respectively. Title pages will be prepared in manuscript.

(2)

Army Form C. 2118.

WAR DIARY
or
~~INTELLIGENCE SUMMARY~~.
(Erase heading not required.)

2nd Bn Irish Guards.

Place	Date	Hour	Summary of Events and Information	Remarks and references to Appendices
	~~Sept 16th~~		~~Battalion drill and P.T. B.T. in the morning~~	
CRIEL PLAGE	Sept 16th		A Brigade Route march. Each Bn was commanded by a Captain and the drums marched at the head of their respective Battalion. They did not however all play at once. The whole Brigade were able to muster a strong Company.	
	Sept 17th		Coys were at the disposal of their Coy Commanders during the morning for march discipline close order drill etc. Spray baths were declared open.	
	Sept 18th		Sunday. Usual services in the morning. In the afternoon the Battalion tug o war team proceeded to DIEPPE to take part in a competition which they won with consummate ease. There was a protest against their weight but it was disallowed there being no weighing machine to prove it.	

A5834 Wt. W4973/M687 750,000 8/16 D. D. & L. Ltd. Forms/C.2118/13

Instructions regarding War Diaries and Intelligence Summaries are contained in F. S. Regs., Part II. and the Staff Manual respectively. Title pages will be prepared in manuscript.

(3) Army Form C. 2118.

WAR DIARY
or
~~INTELLIGENCE SUMMARY.~~
(Erase heading not required.)

2nd Bn. Irish Guards.

Place	Date	Hour	Summary of Events and Information	Remarks and references to Appendices
CREE PLACE	Sept 9th		No. 2 & 4 Coys paraded for Lewis Gun instruction [illegible] No. 1 & 3 Coys paraded at the same time for bombing. All available NCOs did map reading under Captain Law. In the afternoon the Battalion [illegible] on the range. In the evening a Kana [illegible] Concert party gave a most excellent entertainment. The Commanding Officer returned off leave and took over command from Major Nugent, who proceeded on leave the next morning.	
	Sept 10th		Coys were on the range in the morning for two hours each. When not on the range they did Drill and Lewis Gun instruction.	
	Sept 11th		Coys paraded in the morning for P.T. & B.T. at 8 am. for Bombing at 9.15 for Lewis Gun instruction at 10.15 & for Drill at 11.30	

A5834 Wt. W4973/M687 750,000 8/16 D. D. & L. Ltd. Forms/C.2118/13

Army Form C. 2118.

(4)

Instructions regarding War Diaries and Intelligence Summaries are contained in F. S. Regs., Part II. and the Staff Manual respectively. Title pages will be prepared in manuscript.

WAR DIARY
or
~~INTELLIGENCE SUMMARY~~.
(Erase heading not required.)

2nd Bn Irish Guards.

Place	Date	Hour	Summary of Events and Information	Remarks and references to Appendices
[illegible] PLACE	Sept 12th		Coys did drill, Lewis Gun instruction and P&BT in the morning. N.C.O.s did a scheme under their Coy Commanders. The Baths were allotted to the Battalion.	
	Sept 13th		Another Brigade Route march, similar to last week.	
	Sept 14th		P&BT, Bombing and drill for the Companies. N.C.O.s attended class under the Sgt Major.	
	Sept 15th		Sunday. Usual Divine Service. The Commanding Officer inspected Camp after Church.	
	Sept 16th		Lewis Gun instruction and firing for the whole Battalion during the morning. In the afternoon we proceeded to the range.	
	Sept 17th		Range all the morning. In the evening the Divisional Pierrot troupe (3rd Bn Coldstream Guards) gave a performance at the theatre [illegible], which was well [illegible] the	

A5834 Wt. W4973/M687 750,000 8/16 D. D. & L. Ltd. Forms/C.2118/13

Army Form C. 2118.

(5)

Instructions regarding War Diaries and Intelligence Summaries are contained in F. S. Regs., Part II. and the Staff Manual respectively. Title pages will be prepared in manuscript.

WAR DIARY
or
~~INTELLIGENCE SUMMARY.~~
(Erase heading not required.)

2nd Bn [illegible] March.

Place	Date	Hour	Summary of Events and Information	Remarks and references to Appendices
			standard of these excellent [illegible] [illegible] fooling.	
[illegible]	Sept [illegible]		Daily bombing & Lewis Gun instruction & PT BT for all Coys during the morning. All NCOs [illegible] also paraded for an interesting discourse on the German Light machine gun by the Armourer Sergeant.	
	Sept [illegible]		[illegible] SBR drill, Drill and PT BT during the morning. A Battalion Harriers Club was started.	
	Sept [illegible]		Brigade Route March. Capt [illegible] commanded the Column, Capt Dane-Longworth the [illegible]. An Epidemic of foot and mouth disease having broken out near by all milk has to be boiled.	

A5834 Wt. W4973/M687 750,000 8/16 D. D. & L. Ltd. Forms/C.2118/13

(6)

Army Form C. 2118.

Instructions regarding War Diaries and Intelligence Summaries are contained in F. S. Regs., Part II. and the Staff Manual respectively. Title pages will be prepared in manuscript.

WAR DIARY
or
INTELLIGENCE SUMMARY.
(Erase heading not required.)

2nd Bn Irish Guards.

Place	Date	Hour	Summary of Events and Information	Remarks and references to Appendices
CRIEL PLAGE	Sept 22nd		P & BT, Drill and SBR parade Coys during the morning. Lewis Gun instruction and firing, drill under the Sgt Major for NCOs. Baths were allotted to the Battalion.	
	Sept 23rd		Sunday. Usual Services. The Commanding Officer inspected Camp after Church.	
	Sept 23rd		Usual routine in the morning. There was a most excellent lecture on Tanks by Major Boyd Rochfort.	
	Sept 24th		The 4th Bn Grenadier Guards and the 3rd Bn Coldstream Guards left CRIEL PLAGE to fight. The 2nd Bn Irish Guards thus were left in sole possession.	
	Sept 25th		All NCOs parade at CRIEL CHURCH for a tactical scheme.	

A5834 Wt. W4973/M687 750,000 8/16 D. D. & L. Ltd. Forms/C.2118/13

Instructions regarding War Diaries and Intelligence Summaries are contained in F. S. Regs., Part II. and the Staff Manual respectively. Title pages will be prepared in manuscript.

(7)

WAR DIARY
or
INTELLIGENCE SUMMARY.
(*Erase heading not required.*)

2nd Bn Irish Guards

Army Form C. 2118.

Place	Date	Hour	Summary of Events and Information	Remarks and references to Appendices
[illegible]	Sept 26th		Battalion paraded in drill order in garden for drill and at 10.30 am for Lewis Gun instruction. All NCOs did map reading under Captain W.E. Munford MC.	H.R. Alexander Maj. Comdg 2nd Bn. Irish Guards. 3/10/18
	Sept 27th		The Battalion moved over to the Camp lately vacated by the 3rd Bn Coldstream Guards. Work was done in fitting in & generally setting things straight.	
	Sept 28th		Battalion did [illegible] drill in the morning. At 10.15 am they had Lewis Gun instruction on the YEAUVILLE RANGE.	
	Sept 29th		Sunday. Usual Services. Commanding Officer inspected camp after church.	
	Sept 30th		Dr Alexander Irvine came and lectured to the attached Officers on "America and the War". An unmitigated success. In the evening a very choice concert was given by the attached Officers.	

A5834 Wt. W4973/M687 750,000 8/16 D. D. & L. Ltd. Forms/C.2118/13

CONFIDENTIAL.

W A R   D I A R Y

of

2nd Battalion, Irish Guards.

Vol. X - 1918. --

PERIOD :

From 1st October

To 31st October, 1918.

----

0 4 7 0 9 5

2nd Bn. Irish Guards.

Army Form C. 2118.

Instructions regarding War Diaries and Intelligence Summaries are contained in F. S. Regs., Part II. and the Staff Manual respectively. Title pages will be prepared in manuscript.

WAR DIARY
or
~~INTELLIGENCE~~ SUMMARY.

(Erase heading not required.)

Place	Date	Hour	Summary of Events and Information	Remarks and references to Appendices
CRIEL PLAGE	Oct 1st		Coys paraded for an hours drill in the morning and also went on the range for firing practice.	
	Oct 2nd		All NCO's paraded under Captain James-Longworth for map reading. The rest of the Battalion paraded for drill under the adjutant	
	Oct 3rd		The Commanding Officer inspected companies in clothing Equipment etc. For the rest of the morning Coys were at the disposal of Coy Commanders. All NCO's attended a tactical lecture	
	Oct 4th		all NCO's proceeded on a tactical scheme with No 3 Young Officers Company. The rest of the Bn did drill, gas drill etc	
	Oct 5th		All the Young Officers departed to join their Bn amidst mutual expressions of goodwill. The Bn did steady drill and the NCO's were examined	

A7092). Wt. W12839/M1293 750,000. 1/17. D. D & L., Ltd. Forms/C2118/14.

Instructions regarding War Diaries and Intelligence Summaries are contained in F. S. Regs., Part II. and the Staff Manual respectively. Title pages will be prepared in manuscript.

WAR DIARY
or
~~INTELLIGENCE SUMMARY.~~
(Erase heading not required.)

Army Form C. 2118.

Place	Date	Hour	Summary of Events and Information	Remarks and references to Appendices
			by the Commanding Officer in mapreading tactics etc. Their knowledge was scanty.	
Rifle Pt C[illegible]	Oct 6th		Sunday. Usual Divine Services were held for Roman Catholics. The Church of England contingent however were denied the benefits of worship as the Chaplain entrusted with the care of their spiritual welfare had departed with the Brigade and failed to make any arrangement for any services.	
	Oct 7th		The Commanding Officer started a series of lectures to NCO's, the first one being on Outposts. He also did an outpost scheme with them. The remainder of the Bn did open order drill and Lewis Gun instruction	
	Oct 8th		The Commanding Officer gave a lecture on mapreading	

T2134. Wt. W708—776. 500000. 4/15. Sir J. C. & S.

Army Form C. 2118.

Instructions regarding War Diaries and Intelligence Summaries are contained in F. S. Regs., Part II. and the Staff Manual respectively. Title pages will be prepared in manuscript.

WAR DIARY
or
~~INTELLIGENCE SUMMARY.~~

(Erase heading not required.)

Place	Date	Hour	Summary of Events and Information	Remarks and references to Appendicees
CRIZ PLACE			to the NCO's, followed by a scheme – The remainder of the Bn did Lewis Gun instruction and drill.	
	Oct 9th		The Commanding Officer lectured to the NCO's on Advanced Guards followed by a scheme in which the whole Battalion took part. In the afternoon the "2nd Bn Irish Guards Harriers Club" went for their weekly training run. The Commanding Officer took them out for about 2½ miles at a steady pace. They then raced home –	
	Oct 10th		The Battalion went to the "POLYGONE" range for firing practice. A special order of the day was issued by GOC 4th ARMY to the effect that all peace talk must cease.	
	Oct 11th		The Commanding Officer held an examination for all	

T2134. Wt. W708–776. 500000. 4/15. Sir J. C. & S.

Instructions regarding War Diaries and Intelligence Summaries are contained in F. S. Regs., Part II. and the Staff Manual respectively. Title pages will be prepared in manuscript.

WAR DIARY
or
~~INTELLIGENCE SUMMARY.~~
(Erase heading not required.)

Army Form C. 2118.

Place	Date	Hour	Summary of Events and Information	Remarks and references to Appendices
CRIEL PLAGE			NCO's in tactics & mapreading. A considerable improvement was noticed in their knowledge. The 2nd in Command also examined them in drill. The Commanding Officer proceeded in the afternoon to go stay with Colonel Gilbert Hamilton Grenadier Guards, Commanding 2nd Army School, in order to visit the FLANDERS Battlefield.	
	Oct 12th		Coys were at the disposal of Coy Commanders for inspections etc and also did 1½ hours Lewis Gun instruction.	
	Oct 13th		Sunday. Usual Divine Services for Roman Catholics. No Service for Church of England for the same reasons as mentioned in my entry of the 6th inst.	

Instructions regarding War Diaries and Intelligence Summaries are contained in F. S. Regs., Part II. and the Staff Manual respectively. Title pages will be prepared in manuscript.

WAR DIARY
or
~~INTELLIGENCE~~ SUMMARY.
(Erase heading not required.)

Army Form C. 2118.

Place	Date	Hour	Summary of Events and Information	Remarks and references to Appendices
Criel Plage	Oct 14th		The 2nd in command gave a lecture to all NCO's on artillery formation followed by a demonstration. In the evening the Bn received a sore blow as a memo arrived ordering the Commanding Officer to proceed to take up command of the Xth Corps School.	
	Oct 15th		The Battalion shot on the POLYGONE Range in the morning. The Commanding Officer returned from his tour of the line in the evening.	
	Oct 16th		Coys were at the Disposal of Company Commanders in the morning. The Baths were also allotted to Coys.	
	Oct 17th		Musketry on the range in the morning. In the afternoon a Battalion Cross Country race was	

Instructions regarding War Diaries and Intelligence Summaries are contained in F. S. Regs., Part II. and the Staff Manual respectively. Title pages will be prepared in manuscript.

WAR DIARY
or
~~INTELLIGENCE SUMMARY.~~
(Erase heading not required.)

Army Form C. 2118.

Place	Date	Hour	Summary of Events and Information	Remarks and references to Appendices
ORIEL PLACE	0		held. A good stiff course of about 5 miles was laid out and a field of about 35 got away at 2.30 pm. Sgt Gilmartin took the lead at once close followed by Cpl J. M. Hills and Cpl Birch. This order was maintained for the first 2 miles. Sgt Gilmartin who was suffering from a sprained foot then dropped behind and Timmey came into third place. The first 3 kept together for the remainder of the journey ~~when~~ but Cpl Hills with a magnificent sprint went away about 200 yards from home and won comfortably by about 30 yards. Cpl Birch being second Timmey 3rd, Sgt Bayley 4th and Sgt Gilmartin 5th.	
	Oct 1st		The Commanding Officer proceeded to take up his new appointment. The whole Bn turned out to see him off and say Goodbye to him. Never before has any	

A7092). Wt. W12839/M1293. 750,000. 1/17. D. D & L., Ltd. Forms/C2118/14.

Instructions regarding War Diaries and Intelligence Summaries are contained in F. S. Regs., Part II. and the Staff Manual respectively. Title pages will be prepared in manuscript.

WAR DIARY
or
~~INTELLIGENCE SUMMARY.~~
(Erase heading not required.)

Army Form C. 2118.

Place	Date	Hour	Summary of Events and Information	Remarks and references to Appendices
			Commanding Officer had a more enthusiastic and loyal send off. He left a letter to be published in orders saying goodbye to the B^n, in which he said "In bidding you farewell I wish to express to you all my sincere grief at leaving a Battalion I am so fond of. We have been through some hard times together but the remembrance of those battles in which the 2nd B^n has taken such a glorious part will always be a great pride to me. Remember the great name this wonderful Battalion has made for itself in the war. Be proud of it and guard it jealously. I leave you with complete confidence that its reputation is safe in your hands. I thank you from the bottom of my heart for the loyalty you have always shown me during the whole time that I have had the honour of commanding you.	
			I wish you all and individually the best possible luck and success, and a safe return to your homes	

A7092). Wt. W12839/M1297. 750,000. 1/17. D. D & L., Ltd. Forms/C2118/14.

Instructions regarding War Diaries and Intelligence Summaries are contained in F. S. Regs., Part II. and the Staff Manual respectively. Title pages will be prepared in manuscript.

WAR DIARY
or
~~INTELLIGENCE SUMMARY.~~
(Erase heading not required.)

Army Form C. 2118.

Place	Date	Hour	Summary of Events and Information	Remarks and references to Appendices
			when the war is won". Never has a Battalion had a finer man or a greater Commanding Officer.	
CRIEL PLAGE	Oct 19th		The Battalion fired on the Polygone range during the morning.	
	Oct 20th		Sunday. Still no divine service for the Church of England. The Commanding Officer inspected camp during the morning.	
	Oct 21st		The Commanding Officer gave a lecture on rear guards to the NCO's. The remainder of the Bn did Lewis Gun instruction and drill	
	Oct 22nd		The ~~Commanders~~ Companies did 1 hours drill under their Company Commanders. The rest of the morning was spent in Lewis Gun instruction. NCO's had a lecture on map reading	

A7092). Wt. W12839/M1293. 750,000. 1/17. D. D & L., Ltd. Forms/C2118/14.

Instructions regarding War Diaries and Intelligence Summaries are contained in F. S. Regs., Part II. and the Staff Manual respectively. Title pages will be prepared in manuscript.

WAR DIARY

or

~~INTELLIGENCE~~ SUMMARY.

(Erase heading not required.)

Army Form C. 2118.

Place	Date	Hour	Summary of Events and Information	Remarks and references to Appendices
CRIL PLAGE	Oct 23rd		The Commanding Officer took all NCO's out on a mapreading scheme in the morning. The rest of the Bn did Saluting drill In the afternoon the "Harriers" went for a run. News arrived at about 4 pm that the 4th Guards Brigade were returning in a few days. Steps were at once taken to get camps ready for their arrival.	
	Oct 24th		Work was carried on pitching tents, etc in the lines of the 4th Bn Grenadier Guards and 3rd Bn Coldstream Guards. Mons MOUQUET, official interpreter to the 3rd Bn Coldstream Guards, visited the Bn in the afternoon and remained to dinner.	
	Oct 25th		The Bn moved back to their old camp in the morning as they had occupied that of the 3rd Bn Coldstream Gds during their absence. The rest of the day was occupied by putting up marquees etc	

Army Form C. 2118.

Instructions regarding War Diaries and Intelligence Summaries are contained in F. S. Regs., Part II. and the Staff Manual respectively. Title pages will be prepared in manuscript.

WAR DIARY
or
~~INTELLIGENCE SUMMARY.~~
(Erase heading not required.)

Place	Date	Hour	Summary of Events and Information	Remarks and references to Appendices
CRIEL PLAGE	Oct 26th		The Brigade arrived in the morning. Our drums met Bns and ~~marched~~ played them into camp. Tea was issued to them on arrival.	
	Oct 27th		Sunday. Usual Divine Services. In the afternoon the headquarter officers ~~[illegible]~~ & Company Commanders played a football match against the warrant officers and staff sergeants of the Bn. A good game resulted in a win for the officers by 3 goals to 2.	
	Oct 28th		The Bn shot on the 'POLYGONE' range in the morning. In the afternoon No 2 Coy played against No 3 Coy in the 1st round of the intercompany competition. The result was a draw 2 goals all.	
	Oct 29th		The Battalion paraded for drill from 8.30 am – 9.30 for P & BT from 10 – 11 and for Lewis Gun instruction from	

A7092). Wt. W12839/M1293. 750,000. 1/17. D. D & L., Ltd. Forms/C2118/14.

Instructions regarding War Diaries and Intelligence Summaries are contained in F. S. Regs., Part II. and the Staff Manual respectively. Title pages will be prepared in manuscript.

WAR DIARY
or
INTELLIGENCE SUMMARY.
(Erase heading not required.)

Army Form C. 2118.

Place	Date	Hour	Summary of Events and Information	Remarks and references to Appendices
			11-30 am – 12-30 pm. ~~In the afternoon~~	
	Oct 30th		The Bn went for a route march of about 10 miles in the morning. In the afternoon H&Rs played the Drums in the first round of the competition. The result was a draw.	
	Oct 31st		Coys paraded for drill, gas drill, Lewis Gun instruction during the morning. The NCO's went on a map reading scheme with the Commanding Officer. ~~A pa~~ Instructions as to training Lewis Gunners was issued ~~to Bn to Bns~~; amongst others that Each class would have an instructor!	

E.J. Nugent Major
Commanding 2nd Bn Irish Guards.

A7092 Wt. W128.9/M1293 750,000. 1/17. D. D & L. Ltd. Forms/C2118/14.

www.ingramcontent.com/pod-product-compliance
Lightning Source LLC
Chambersburg PA
CBHW081432160426
43193CB00013B/2264
* 9 7 8 1 4 7 4 5 0 2 1 4 6 *